Praise for *The Indomitable Elizabeth Fries Ellet – Feminist*

"In Vicki Pellar Price's book, she presents, through documents and with thoughtful scholarship, the great swirl of Elizabeth Fries Ellet's life. Ellet was a writer, a fighter for white women's rights, a compatriot of many 19th century women of a certain class, all of whom had to deal with the lack of equal rights in all fields: domestic, academic, publishing, and marriage. This book deals in dizzying detail with the place E.A. Poe held in society, and in writing circles, and how his favor was sought by many women because of his power as arbiter of quality writing and his ability to assist in careers being launched. The story of Ellet also touches on the Abolitionist movement, early feminism, how libel and slander traveled through correspondence, rumor, and lies. Ellet, despite being presented by Poe in such negative ways, prevailed as a writer, publishing many books, and fought for women's rights and freedoms in her life. Our thanks to Pellar Price for this carefully researched look at a precise time and set of characters in American history."

–Deborah Keenan, author of eleven poetry collections

"This was a textbook and thorough dissertation on the treatment of women and especially strong women who defend women's rights, like Elizabeth Ellet. The fact that there is a society like the Poe society that defends Edgar Allen Poe's misogyny, narcissism and attacks on women today shows that women have made little progress in the battle for rights. It is a great history of women who blazed the trail in defense of Women's Rights and were good writers who did not receive the acclaim they deserved. This should be reading for High School and College History as well as on anyone's list to read who is interested in learning more about Women's Issues from a historic perspective and the stereotypes still perpetrated."

–Sharon Borine, President of the League of Women Voters, Minnetonka, Eden Prairie, Hopkins (MEPH)

"In an era when remnants of old English Femme Covert law's vice-like grip on women's rights dominated American women in society, along came Elizabeth Fries Ellet, a prolific historian, populist writer, feminist, naturalist author, influencer, and transformational activist for the advancement of women. Pellar Price's important, scholarly writing reveals the systematic failure of chauvinistic, misogynist male historians who trivialized and ignored brilliant women like Ellet. Ellet should be right up there with the other great historians of her day."

–Betty Folliard, former Minnesota State Legislator and Founder, of ERA Minnesota

The Indomitable
Elizabeth Fries Ellet – Feminist

Wisdom Editions

Minneapolis

Cover art by Vicki Pellar Price
Cover and book design by Gary Lindberg

The Indomitable
Elizabeth Fries Ellet – Feminist

Defining the Historical Truth of the Nineteenth Century

Vicki Pellar Price

Wisdom
Editions

Minneapolis

In memory and admiration…
Elizabeth Fries Ellet 1812, 1818-1877

It appears Ellet was more than the Nineteenth Century men in her literary circles could handle. Ellet married an educated man whose accomplishments and stature are overlooked, nevertheless he allowed her to seek her own career. She was devoted to him and wrote about his illness and death to a dear friend. Ellet, like Ann S. Stephens, Margaret Fuller, Amelia Bloomer and others were all committing a revolutionary act by writing about women's travails in an era in which women gradually broke away from writing posthumously. Bloomer edited the first women's magazine, the Lily. Like Ellet, they wrote about women, defended women. Ellet also defended women wearing pants, named after Amelia Bloomer, who was involved with the women's rights and temperance movement, and advocated for women's dress reform. A first, pants named after her were called bloomers for women to wear underneath shorter dresses. Ellet broke with separate spheres and ventured out in ways that infuriated her literary male counterparts. Femininity vs. feminist, Poe and Griswold et al, most men of that era preferred the former, which exemplifies a war of words still ongoing today.

Table of Contents

Prologue

Elizabeth Fries Ellet and her literary female contemporaries began reordering the 19th-century social stature of women, a story of females striving for their independence that cannot be contained within a set of interpretive signs on a trail at the Richard T. Anderson Conservation Area, adjacent to the Minnesota River. In not-so-subtle ways for a 19th century woman, Ellet, like female authors of the 18th and 19th century, rebelled against strict gender roles of females and female writers. The reality is that 21st-century women still share in some of Ellet's travails in claiming their own freedoms.

Elizabeth Fries Ellet

In an era of misogyny and few women's rights, female authors and feminists like Ellet endured the battles of the 19th century to not only claim their right to authorship, but their rights as females. Ellet fought that fight along with the most renowned women in our history.

Elizabeth Fries Lummis Ellet

Chapter 1

Beginnings: Fore Fathers, Fore Mothers

History and legacy informed every fiber of Elizabeth Fries Ellet's life. Born in 1812-1818, Ellet was the daughter of William Nixon Lummis, a prominent physician who studied medicine in Philadelphia under Dr. Benjamin Rush, who was a Founding Father and a signee of the United States Declaration of Independence. Lummis married Sara Maxwell after Elizabeth's mother died in 1812. She is named after her mother, Elizabeth Fries Ellet.

Sara Maxwell's father joined the army of General George Washington as captain of a company of 100 volunteers known as Maxwell's Company, named after Ellet's father's second wife, Sara Maxwell. John Maxwell was a Revolutionary War captain, who was the lieutenant of the first company raised in Sussex County, New Jersey. He later joined the army of General George Washington, as captain of a company of 100 volunteers known as Maxwell's Company. Maxwell was an Irish-born brigadier general *in the Continental Army during the American Revolutionary War*. Washington chose him to command a group of men who would become known as Maxwell's Brigade. Maxwell was elected to his position by Congress on Oct. 23, 1776. Due to their exemplary service, Maxwell's Brigade is said to have been the first to fly the Stars and Stripes in battle during the Philadelphia Campaign in 1777-78. The British overtook the American capital city of Philadelphia, Pennsylvania, where the Founders fought for American Independence. With the help of the French, Washington was able to defeat the British at Yorktown.

Ellet spent her youth at the Pulteney Estate in Sodus Bay, New York, growing up in a rebuilt house originally erected during the Revolutionary War at a time when Seneca and Cayuga Indians lived in Sodus Bay before Europeans invaded their homeland. Elizabeth's father, Dr. Henry Nixon Lummis was a wealthy landowner who purchased the Pulteney Estate, hundreds of acres of land in New York State, that originally belonged to the Indians before the Revolutionary War. These foundational connections likely were the impetus that compelled Ellet to recover the historical truth about women who participated in the American Revolution.

The war ended in 1783 with the Treaty of Paris. Elizabeth was born in 1818, though some say earlier in 1812, a year the war further impacted America's future. The United Kingdom established a northern boundary in the Treaty of 1818 between the U.S. and the United Kingdom, which established the northern boundary as the 49th parallel of the U.S, in what was then British North America, and now Canada.

What the aftermath of the Revolutionary War brought were changes that are still in process. An organized abolitionist movement was born, and English traditions were eliminated. Since the Church of England was the Anglican church in America, that too was dispensed with. Throughout texts of thousands of words, the Declaration of Independence 1776 and the United States Constitution, 1787, our current presence is revealed to us through our past, while learning that the people who were exempt from equal treatment in our nation's early days, slaves, black men and black women and women of all colors and ethnicities, despite movements for change experienced throughout our history, are still present today.

Elizabeth Fries Ellet defied the status-quo of what came to be known as separate spheres, one in which men lived unencumbered, while women's roles were defined by men. Imagining her standing among us today, no quill pens and ink pots, instead email and computers, no horses and carriages, instead airplanes and cars, and imaginings of double her literary output from someone whose life was dedicated to words that defined women's lives.

As a girl Elizabeth attended the Aurora Female Seminary in Aurora New York. Her upbringing was in the tradition of the 19th-century role into which women of privilege were born, that women should be educated, so far as it supported their duties within the home: caring for children, running a household, and understanding their gender role in society.

Being a writer was not an acceptable role for women in that era, but Ellet followed the passions of women before her, who were adept at crafting words into images of 18th and 19th-century life, some who wrote anonymously under male pseudonyms in order to be accepted and then published posthumously. In 1834, Ellet translated Silvio Pellico's Euphemio of Messina and published it anonymously. Her first published book, *Poems, Translated and Original,* translated by Ellet from Spanish, German, French and Italian, demonstrated her fluency in foreign languages and was published in 1835 at the age of sixteen. Her poem *Sodus Bay* is still featured at Historic Sodus Bay Pointe online. A Tragedy in Five Acts *Teresa Contarini*, which was included in Ellet's *Poems, translated and Original*, had a successful theater run in New York and other cities. Ellet wrote the *Characters of Schiller* in 1839, the *Scenes in the Life of Joanna of Sicily* and *Rambles About the Country*, in 1840 and in 1848 she began research for *The Women of the American Revolution,* which was written in two volumes, with a third volume added in 1850. In 1849, she published *Evenings at Woodlawn,* in 1850 the *Domestic History of the American Revolution*, in 1852, *Pioneer Women of the West* and *Summer Rambles in the West* and in 1859 *Women Artists in All Ages and Countries* was published in 1859. This list doesn't include other books and all the many stories, poems in Godey's Lady's Book, the Broadway Journal, stories in Dime Novels. Ellet was also an editor at a New York Evening Press newspaper.

Chapter 2

A Leap of Destiny from South Carolina
Back to New York, Elizabeth's Letter
to Mary Balmanno, English Writer,
Editor, and Illustrator, On William
Henry Ellet's Death

At seventeen Ellet married chemist Dr. William Henry Ellet in 1835, a graduate of Columbia College in New York who pursued medical studies, gaining a gold medal for a dissertation on the compounds of cyanogen, a colorless and highly toxic gas.

They moved to South Carolina where he was a professor of chemistry, mineralogy, and geology at South Carolina College in 1836. Dr. Ellet is also known to have experimented in the early days of photography on a Daguerreotype process with Aaron Denman Chaloner, a medical student in Philadelphia; chemist and artist John Jay Mapes in New York City, professor of chemistry and pharmacy John Locke in Cincinnati; which included William Henry Ellet, who was living in South Carolina at the time. These documented experiments in America (all dating from the spring of 1839) did not survive, but the "circumstances were recorded and mentioned in periodicals and reports and in recollections later penned by informed parties."

Dr. Ellet, along with receiving a gold medal for a dissertation on the compounds of cyanogen, also was recognized for his discovery of a new and inexpensive means of preparing guncotton, which used cotton dipped *in a mixture of nitric and sulfuric acids* to make gun powder. He was presented with a service of silver plate for the new discovery of a cheap method of preparing gun cotton. Dr. Ellet became a professor of experimental chemistry at Columbia College in 1835 and professor of geology at South Carolina College in 1830.

While living in South Carolina Ellet published in the *Southern Literary Journal and Monthly Magazine* and *Southern Literary Messenger*, though she still wrote for national magazines and newspapers, including the Democratic Review, New Yorker, Harpers and Union Magazine. Ellet also wrote *The Characters of Schiller* (1839), *Scenes in the Life of Joanna Sicily* (1840) and *Rambles about the Country* (1840), a travelogue of observations while traveling around the country, and she also wrote poetry and essays while in South Carolina.

Important dates are still disputed as to Elizabeth's and her husband's departure from South Carolina. The following is correct according to the Duycinick Family Papers at the NYPL, Mrs. Ellet and her husband both left South Carolina together in 1849 for New York and remained there permanently and Dr. Ellet accepted a position at the Manhattan Gas Company in 1852. He held that office until his death in 1859.

The 1849 date likely refers to selling their house in South Carolina and moving back to New York together. This is revealed in "letters written by William Henry Ellet to Timothy Green and John Mitchell regarding the sale of property in South Carolina and the wishes of his wife Elizabeth to leave the South." *William Henry Ellet Papers, New York Public Library.* It's also included in the *William Henry Ellet Papers, University of South Carolina.*

The following dates that don't correlate with either the *Duycinick Family Papers, New York Public Library* or the *William Henry Ellet Papers, University of South Carolina*, are everywhere. In Sandra L. Langer's *Review of Women Artists in all Ages and Countries*, Elizabeth Fries Ellet, Harper & Co, 1859, it's written that William Henry

Ellet and his wife Elizabeth Fries Ellet left South Carolina together in 1848, (1850 also attributed to this move) moving back to New York and he accepted employment as a consulting chemist of the Manhattan gas company in 1852. It's likely that Ellet, who traveled back and forth from South Carolina to New York, did so frequently and that her husband may have also done so, as he was looking for a job in New York.

Dr Ellet came to the conclusion that his wife was desirous of leaving South Carolina, so he agreed, despite his success teaching at Columbia, he promised to accept the "first good situation" that would materialize in another city. Despite his laudable accomplishments, Ellet's husband remains but a footnote in her larger legacy as a prolific female writer, including her singular contribution to women's history, with *The Women of the American Revolution* in three volumes, when only male writers dominated that genre.

Ellet frequently traveled back and forth between South Carolina and New York City, visiting her home town, Sodus Bay and trips she took across the country resulted in two books, *Summer Rambles about the Country* and *Summer Rambles in the West*. She stayed with friends in New York temporarily on her initial arrival. Also, after nursing her husband Dr. Ellet until his death, she stayed with a friend and her brother to gain distance from her sorrow.

In a long letter to Mary Balmanno, an English writer, editor and illustrator who moved to New York with her husband, and a friend, Ellet wrote of the transition after her husband's death, having to leave their apartment, while visiting and staying with one friend because the associations were too sad. She wrote she couldn't remain where they had lived together. She moved in with her brother, feeling unsettled, taking over the children's rooms, until she could find a place of her own, after Dr. Ellet's death. She wrote, "I miss sadly the care and attention I devoted to my husband for years until his death." She never gave up her place as his caretaker, he made her pray with him continually, and Christian friends came too and prayed with them. The letter in the Duycinick Papers, NYPL, is a verification that Ellet's faith was strong and her devotion to her husband was real.

Yet, In *Pursuit of Possibility, Elizabeth Ellet and the Women of the American Revolution*, a Master of Arts thesis by Gretchen Ferris Schoel, she cites an Edgar Allen Poe letter to Sarah Helen Whitman, 24 November 1848, in which she describes a woman that none of the New York.

Bluestocking ladies would recognize. This was the view from Poe, in a dissertation by Schoel about Ellet's religiosity! What Schoel might not have known is Ellet's side of the story, that Ellet was religious, she converted from being an Episcopalian to Catholicism, later in life. To corroborate Ellet's religiosity, Kenneth Silverman, author of *Edgar A. Poe, A Biography, Mournful And Never-Ending Remembrance,* referred to Ellet as a "zealous Christian" with "strict religious observances, unblemished moral training and conservative ideas."

School wrote, "Yet those who knew Ellet well would never have called her "pious. For while extolling feminine goodness in her published writings, Ellet was often quite unprincipled in her private life. Her whole study, throughout life," Edgar Allan Poe avowed, "[had] been the gratification of her malignity. Having once been entangled in a suspiciously prurient relationship with Poe, Ellet exhibited a puerile jealousy when her arch-rival, Frances Sargeant (is misspelled by Schoel) Osgood, charmed away the licentious Poe." This interpretation is not supported by Kenneth Silverman, Pulitzer Prize winner, who wrote in "Edgar A. Poe, A Biography, Mournful and Never-Ending Remembrance," his summation untainted by the Poe Society, was that the earlier relationship between Poe and Ellet and Poe's temporary disinterest in Osgood, while being taken-away with Ellet, made Osgood jealous.

Edgar Allen Poe

With brilliance, a troubled heart, bias chauvinism and the desire for his work to be known and admired, Poe wielded 19th Century spheres in ways that did not go unnoticed by those he criticized and maligned the most.

Edgar Allan Poe

What Schoel might not have known when writing her thesis is that a letter Ellet wrote to Poe about the unjust removal of Dr. Robert Henry, then President of South Carolina College, for him to use in an article in the Broadway Journal, at the time Poe was editor, publisher. There was a fragment alluding to a romantic interest in Poe that was not written in Ellet's hand. The portion of her letter that was written in her hand spoke about being concerned that her husband wouldn't approve of her writing the piece. On a separate fragment note in German asking Poe, supposedly seductively, to call for a letter was a fake. The Poe Society/Blog ultimately conceded that part of the letter was not written by Ellet, "on the back of the letter in an unknown hand, the partial and incorrect translation."

Ellet sent Poe a letter asking if Poe would publish a letter about the firing of the President of South Carolina College.

She stated that she could not do it herself, because her husband would not approve. On a separate piece of paper, a note was written in German. Even Pulitzer Prize winner Kenneth Silverman mentioned this in his book. Finally, the Poe conglomerate admitted the letter fragment was not written in Ellet's hand.

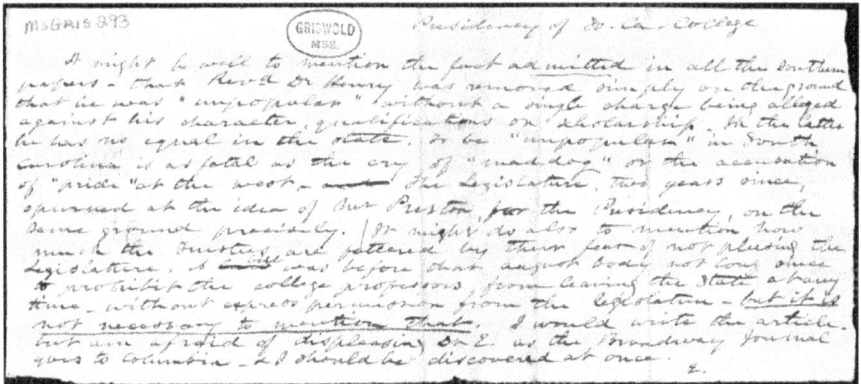

First page of letter from Ellet to Poe

That the Poe behemoth has spent over 150 years impugning Elizabeth Fries Ellet, is so much illusionary fiction, when you consider her circle consisted of leading feminists of the day, fighting for women's rights, who sought her out, knowing her charitable deeds on behalf of women, in what she could be referred to as an underground activist in the fight for women's equality.

It's clear that Ellet was above all else focused on helping women, whether it was about shielding them from their abusive husbands or helping spiritualist Margaret Fox to receive her dowry, Ellet never demonstrated anything other than concern and charitable actions to help protect women. She apologized to Osgood for the gossip that continued to hound her, thereby damaging her reputation. But Ellet couldn't control the behavior of Poe and Osgood, which Ellet had no part in, rather throughout her life she protected women, sometimes resulting in her being the scapegoat. Ultimately, there would have been no gossip if Poe and Griswold had not created the cause of it themselves. Ellet also approached Osgood and a Mrs. Fields, a relative, with an idea to do a book together, demonstrating no malice, no jealousy.

A femme fatale, Osgood's coquettish moves to attain a literary presence enamored both Poe and Griswold. So visible were her intentions that the Osgood and Poe liaisons did not go unnoticed, resulting in a poetic extravaganza and controversy, both still being analyzed today.

Ellet's inroads into the 19th Century New York Literary scene took her away from her husband to pursue writing, which was in and of itself a feminist act. Did she take a train, a carriage, back and forth from South Carolina to New York in either direction? Regardless, we're talking about weeks on dirt roads or over rail tracks. Imagining the courage, the fortitude it took as a female, often on her own, not subscribing to the separate sphere's ideology of men, but in the pursuit of affirming the importance of women having a singular voice and to write for and about women by establishing a feminine voice imprinted in every book she wrote, to do this she ventured out in every realm, every opportunity that availed itself, in what was essentially a man's world.

Frances Sargent Osgood

Not a feminist, Osgood's feminine wiles were coquettish moves to attain a literary presence captivating both Poe and Griswold. Osgood's poems today as compared to the writings of Fuller, Ellet, Sedgwick and all the New York female literati of the 19th century, are out-of-step with women today. What's not outdated is Poe and Osgood's outlasting drama, still enduring via the Poe conglomerate.

Frances Sargent Osgood

Feminism was not Osgood's plight. While most of the New York Bluestocking Literati ladies were writing about sperate spheres; women's rights; issues involving changes brought about by new movements like spiritualism, temperance, female rights, and abolitionism; and simultaneously being right in the midst of a civil war, Osgood was writing love poems to Poe. An outlier, a femme fatal, disengaged from an era of tumultuous change whose flowery romanticism has a smaller audience today.

Ellet was on a considerably different path than most 19th Century women, whose focus was not about the plight of other women. Ellet recognized and penned all the different roles women played, but the role she created for herself was not one of a housewife or a mother. Being a writer and pursuing the literary world in New York was the reason why Ellet departed South Carolina, leaving her husband Dr. Ellet in South Carolina temporarily until they sold their home and Dr. Ellet moved back to New York permanently in 1849. Ellet's decision resulted in feeling detached from the unlimited literary opportunities and sought the bigger arena of opportunities and relationships with writers, poets, and members of the New York literary society and the press. The move facilitated Ellet's first foray into the literary world of esteemed American writers known worldwide.

It wasn't long before the men who ultimately would demean her, became her literary contacts, including Poe, and Griswold. Distinguished writers Lydia Sigourney, Ann Stephens, Catharine Sedgwick, and Margaret Fuller were writers and editors Ellet became acquainted with. Ellet's writing career was blooming as her contacts and friendships grew, she "published, taught, and gave public readings." Before the affair of the letters, according to Gretchen Ferris Schoel's dissertation "In Pursuit of Possibility, Elizabeth Ellet and the Women of the American Revolution" (1992), Ellet "became an intimate friend" of Poe, sought aid and advice from Margaret Fuller and Anne Lynch, and seemed to enjoy the soirees and frivolities of New York cultural life." In 19th century speak, the word "intimate" implied much more than a working relationship as compared to the 17th or 18th centuries when friendship was synonymous with romance, marriage. Whatever infatuation Poe may have had in the early stages of their relationship, as described by Kenneth Silverman in his book, *Edgar Allen Poe, A Biography, Mournful and Never-Ending Remembrance,* it was short lived. A more accurate describer is that it was one of opportunity for Ellet and likely beyond her unending literary value to him, until it became clear he may have valued her up until their relationship became contentious. However, Schoel frequently used the Poe Society as a source, in defense of Poe, which is the least unbiased source where Ellet is concerned.

While emerging into the New York literary scene of soirees and social gatherings in the mid-1840s, Ellet was a free agent, a career woman, not a woman of domesticity as prescribed by the mores of acceptable 19th-century females, dictated by the church and men. What Ellet and her female contemporaries fought for, more than 150 years ago, are what women are fighting for today. Context and perspective are critical indicators in a discussion of how our rights, particularly, women's rights continue to be eroded.

Is this not true today? There are now laws controlling a woman's reproductive rights, and no-fault divorce is likely the next prohibition on a woman's freedom. Divorce didn't become legal until the 1920s, but it was rare. Currently it's Republicans who are protesting no-fault divorce, which stipulates that the filing spouse is not required to show wrongdoing by the other spouse as the reason for dissolution. The GOP espouses so-called conservative ideals that to preserve family is preeminent, with women and men having the same options, but historically and currently, women haven't and don't. How is being forced to have a baby a mutually shared option, when laws are derailing a woman's choice to have or not have a child? The truth is that American family structures have changed immensely, the marriage rate has declined, woman are having fewer children, like everything else, marriage is evolving. Attempts to resurrect separate spheres in the 21st century will result in a similar fight that exemplified the 19th century. It's unquestionable, without using the term separate spheres, the Republican party is revisioning women's place, what she can and can't do, based on certain religious/separate spheres beliefs.

In 1829 New York had a post-quickening law which was a felony, and a pre-quickening law was a misdemeanor. Women were fighting for the right to control their earnings, own property, and take custody of their children in the event of a divorce, before the 19th Amendment. A century after its introduction in 1923, the Equal rights amendment was struck down again in April 2023. By the 1880s criminalization became the norm, which wasn't ended until Roe v. Wade in 1973. Now however, after the Supreme Court overturned Roe v. Wade in 2022, there are new abortion laws nationwide that put women's health at risk. Big picture, context, perspective, it's the same institutions, groups, political parties driving anti-female policies today. All you have to do is look up the best states to be a woman and the voting records of elected officials.

Fact 19th and 20th Century: The 19th Amendment was first introduced to Congress in 1878 and was finally certified 42 years later in 1920.

Fact 19th Century: 1848 At Seneca Falls, New York, 300 women and men sign the *Declaration of Sentiments*, a plea for the end of discrimination against women in all spheres.

Fact 21st Century: The National Women's History Alliance report issued by that commission in 1963 documented discrimination against women in virtually every area of American life.

Fact 21st Century: The Equal Rights Amendment, first drafted by the women's suffrage movement in 1923, sought to end the legal distinctions between men and women in terms of divorce, property, employment, and other matters. In 2023/4, the ERA is still blocked by Republicans.

Chapter 3

Anne Lynch Botta's Literary Soirees,
Godey's Lady's Book

The aftermath of relationships formed at Botta's literary soirees, "The House of Expanding Doors," held at 116 Waverly Place, New York, resulted in Poe's banishment due to his affair of the letters. The literary soirees' popularity culminated with Poe's behavior and subsequent response toward Ellet. In retaliation to Ellet's disclosure of letters of a questionable nature, Poe published Literati critiques in Godey's Lady's Book including most Bluestocking ladies with the exception of Ellet. The Poe Foundation and its subgroups have been defaming Ellet ever since, over one hundred and fifty years later. But the intrigue, lies and scapegoating hasn't ended as you read on, there are twists and turns you would never expect.

In a New Yorker article from September 4, 1936, *That Was New York, Anne Lynch's Salon,* by Mortimer Smith, his retelling one can only assume is coming from sources going back more than 150 years, occurring in 1845-1846. What pertains to Poe and Griswold are depictions so dissimilar to other accounts, more realistic considering what we now know.

Wilmot Griswold, a Baptist parson, turned critic and editor sounds full of respectability, but Griswold was replete in self-importance, as he demonstrated throughout his life as well as a being a consummate womanizer, recognized by Smith and historical writers.

And this from Smith, Fanny Osgood, could be picked out of the crowd because she was the only woman swooning at Poe's feet, which did not go unnoticed by those in attendance, including Thomas Dunn English, American Democratic Party politician, author, editor and magazine editor who had a combative relationship with Poe, literally. The mutual respect Lynch and Fuller once shared in their estimations of Poe and their relationship with him ended when they called on him at Fordham and asked for the packet of letters Osgood had sent him. After that day Poe never returned to Waverly Place.

What's not revealed in Smith's rendition is that Mrs. Maria Clemm, Virginia's Clemm's mother, didn't just show Ellet the letters, she had been entertaining visitors who dropped in for tea and to read the letters, resulting in many women viewing the letters. Interestingly, Elizabeth Fries Ellet is never mentioned in the article.

In Carol Mattingly's *Legacy Profile* of Ellet, she describes the missives attributed to her by Poe as a "trouble maker," maligner," and "scandal maker" the assumption being these actions were based on "jealousy or a taste for scandal mongering,". Ellet's highly respected friends, Margaret Fuller, Ann S. Stephens and Anne C. Lynch (Botta) as well as Lydia Sigourney, Sara Josepha Hale and Jared Sparks, historian, whose advice she sought in writing *The Women of the American Revolution*, did not concur with any of these assertions. Neither did Ellet's involvement with women's rights and abolitionist leaders evoke such condemnations, when Ellet was continuously called upon to come to the assistance of women endangered by their husbands.

One-hundred-sixteen Waverly Place was a fashionable New York district from 1845 to 1846. Poe became editor of the *Broadway Journal*, publishing the work of members of the "Literati of New York." Poe's "The Raven" was published, catapulting him to fame. The publication of "The Raven" and "Literati of New York" coincided with an influx of female writers, mostly women with husbands: Mrs. Anna Cora Mowatt; Mrs. Elizabeth Oakes Smith; Mrs. Mary E. Hewitt; Miss Margaret Fuller; Mrs. Elizabeth F. Ellet; Louisa May Alcott, who was unmarried and was an abolitionist and feminist; as well as other women who became not just fascinated by Poe, but sought him out for publishing opportunities and favorable critiques of their work. Ralph Waldo Emerson, Herman Melville, Horace Greely, editor of the *New York Tribune,* and William Cullen Bryant occasionally dropped in; Margaret Fuller, known for her belief in Transcendentalism and support of women's rights, was a frequent participant, along with Frances Sargent Osgood, known today for her involvement with Poe rather than her poetry.

Writing reviews of participants at the soirees was vogue at the time, and magazines like the *Broadway Journal*, which Poe published and critiqued from 1845 to 1846, for a short time, consisted of the work of most of the Bluestocking females attending Lynch's soirees. Poe's critiques of praise and disapproval of writers appeared in many magazines, newspapers and periodicals at that time. Among authors Poe disapproved of included Longfellow, Hawthorne, Emerson, English and James Fenimore Cooper. Among writers he praised were Frances Sargent Osgood, Sara Josepha Hale, Catharine Sedgwick and Margaret Fuller, Fuller initially, until he became more acquainted with her beliefs, which he vehemently opposed.

Some letters of praise were of a romantic nature, which were exchanged between Poe and Frances Sargent Osgood. Adding context, in America in the 19th century what's referred to as "saucy escort" cards was a common way to flirt. Whether the ladies of the "Literati of New York City" used them or not, what we know, there were letter exchanges, many of which were requests for inclusion in *The Broadway Journal* for positive critiques of their work, many could be considered flirtatious. Osgood and Poe's open flirtation, which included published poems of affection, public meetings, trips, the letters which remain a mystery even today, hurt their reputations, so why else would the Poe Society accuse Ellet of writing compromising letters and to prove it over 150 years later by purchasing Ellet's autograph album? Still the goal of the Poe behemoth is to find anything to discredit Ellet, prove her romantic interest in him, when it was ultimately Poe and Osgood's own behavior that sullied their reputations.

There were also financial relationships with some women who paid upfront to help Mrs. Maria Clemm Poe and Poe's wife Virginia Clemm Poe, when she was ill, and for good reviews of their writing. Poe also sought out Griswold to make insignificant female writers appear far beyond their craft and in turn Poe would reciprocate the favor.

Not long before his death Poe shared his true sentiments about female writers in a letter to Annie Richmond, "From this day forth I shun the pestilential society of literary women. They are a heartless, unnatural, venomous, dishonorable set, with no guiding principle, but inordinate self-esteem." Sentiments that mirror Poe's love, hate propensity, when it came to men or women.

Poe's penchant for beauty, attractiveness of women's flesh, translated into his evaluation of their literary work. More telling is that Poe's idealization of women did not extend to those who represented independence, but rather a vision of beauty that Osgood described on her deathbed as Poe's "chivalric, grace-full, and almost tender reverence with which he invariably approached all women," a statement that has been described as "exemplifying a woman who couldn't see beyond her own narcissism and fatal attraction to Poe."

Contrary to Osgood's perception of Poe's adoration for all women, he exhibited a loutish objection to women who did not fit the role of femme fatale. He demonstrated a violent swing of opinion against Margaret Fuller's writing, from stating her style was one of the very best in 1846 at a time when she was doing book reviews for the New York Tribune. In March of 1849 in a review of Lowell's *A Fable for Critics*, Poe ridiculed Fuller for "overweening conceit and Transcendental inanity."

In Poe's "The Literati of New York City," serialized in various 1846 issues of Godey's, he did a sketch of Margaret Fuller applauding her book, *Woman in the Nineteenth Century* for its originality, then attacked her methodology. His objection was that she inserted personal feelings and universalized the essence of woman's nature, "She judges woman by the heart and the intelligence of herself, but there are not more than one or two Miss Fullers on the whole face of the earth," Poe wrote. Poe's see-saw versions of what he thought about Fuller from his writer, critic assessments, which more often than not typified his romanticist 19th century male, chauvinist view of women, that delineated his character.

Sarah Josepha Hale, known as the first professional successful woman's editor of that era, disagreed. Hale acknowledged that Fuller's work may be "visionary and impracticable," but she believed her book had many useful hints in deflecting Poe's charge that Fuller was masculine. Poe said humanity was divided into men, woman and Margaret Fuller. Poe was not alone in his predominant view that women didn't fit into the male dominated business scheme or anywhere outside of household duties and child care. He even rebuked Osgood for not being an exemplary version of a mother. Whether losing a birth mother, adoptive mother and wife contributed to his lack where women were concerned, it became a literary focus. But not unlike his writing, Poe's death turned into a mystery, until recently when medical experts assessed over 150 years later, he likely died of *encephalitic rabies.*

Depending on Poe's categorization of women, their attractiveness and desirability, those were the ones who were more deserving of publication, while helpmates like Marie Louise Shew, a friend and confidant, was useful in taking care of Virginia Poe and Poe himself during difficult times of illness and poverty, and certainly those women he considered his enemies, ladies who would question his morality, were ridiculed and frowned upon. Rather than the merit of the writer, appearances mattered more.

Poe differentiated Catharine Sedgwick from the other literary ladies, categorizing her within the Knickerbocker circles of Cooper and Bryant as "literary pioneers" with national reputation, while simultaneously disparaging her status "along with the absolute merit of her writing," and reiterating, "Strictly speaking Miss Sedgwick is *not one of the literati* of New York city *[sic] (Literati 1200-2001)*. Poe dismissed Sedgwick, but approved of her third novel, "Hope Leslie" 1829, about the conflict between the British Empire, Colonists, and Native Americans, when he deemed, she "deserved an honored place in American literature," according to the Poe Society.

Interestingly Ellet did not include Miss Sedgwick in her book, *Queens of American Society* because of her own positions and the public criticism of Sedgwick's late social life. Catharine was single. Ellet triangulated between true womanhood and separate spheres, when it came to dating vs courtship, but her concern for Poe's wife, Virginia Clemm Poe, was about relinquishing letters that could be perceived as damaging to Virginia's reputation. As it turns out, the Poe Society has perpetuated what Poe deemed interference by Ellet into a scandal, over 150 years later by purchasing Ellet's autograph album in search of her letters. Similarly, via letters between Griswold and his romantic dalliances, Ellet and Anne S. Stephen, in defense of Griswold's wives, contacted them to relay the knowledge of his indiscretions, so too the list of endeavors Ellet was involved in as she answered the call of Elizabeth Cady Stanton and Susan B. Anthony when it came to women fleeing their husbands due to abuse.

This is Ellet personified, in assessing her actions in response to the behavior of men, especially when she deemed their conduct harmful to women. In the following chapters you will read, with the perspective of time, how Ellet went about protecting women, whether it was Frances Sargent Osgood's reputation or connecting with Lydia Mott, Stanton and Anthony to help women fleeing their abusive husbands or ensuring spiritualist Maggie Fox Kane wasn't denied her dowry by Dr. Elijah Kane, all context for understanding Ellet's motivations when it came to standing up for women, whose rights were being suppressed by men.

Another element in understanding Ellet is that she was never restricted by Mr. Ellet; she was free to pursue her writing in South Carolina and New York. Henry Ellet was concerned his wife wasn't happy there and he promised to find a position in New York, which he did at the Manhattan Gas Company in 1852. Ellet went back to New York and pursued her career. It would seem unlikely, incongruous that Ellet, a woman living in that era, who didn't approve of Sedgwick being single and dating, would approve of married men and married women having affairs or committing bigamy, which certainly applies to Rufus Wilmot Griswold who offered marriage to several women while married to Charlotte Meyers Griswold, his second wife, while also romancing the poet, Alice Carey.

Catharine Maria Sedgwick wrote in 1857, "As slaves must be trained for freedom, so women must be educated for usefulness, independence, and contentment in single life... as a mode of life in which one may serve God and humanity, and thus educate the soul, the great purpose of this short life." Unlike the mostly married women among Botta's bluestocking female attendees, as a single woman addressing the female, single life, Sedgwick was helping to set the stage for women, who would no longer be regarded as either "helpless, joyless, or ridiculous," and that dreaded stigma, "old maid," too "would soon cease to be a stigma, and in the lapse of ages possibly become obsolete."

Catharine Maria Sedgwick was single and that was still an impediment in the 19th century, even when compared to the 17th Century, when women were considered spinsters in their twenties. It wasn't until 1896 when dating became more acceptable. Twenty-four years later the 19th amendment was passed, allowing women to vote, but it was still difficult for black women to vote and Native American women were not considered citizens until 1924. Comparing Sedgwick's positions on women's rights to *Godey's Lady's Book* publisher, Sara Josepha Hale represented a significant difference in attitudes toward women's independence, particularly from both male and religious controls of their freedom. Sarah Josepha Hale, *Godey's Lady's Book* editor, did not subscribe to the ideals of the growing feminist movement embraced by many of the

New York Literati ladies who were published frequently in *Godey's Lady's Book*. They enjoyed a wider audience of women, men and supporters and opponents of women's rights than the feminist magazines of that era.

Today, Sarah Josepha Hale, is viewed as a deterrence, impeding women in the development of feminism, women's rights, through a religious lens that supported separate spheres. Hale wrote in her book, *Woman's Record,* that she sought an educational assistant to the moral progress of society. In the introduction to the second edition of the book, Hale stated that "the right influence of women depends on the moral improvement of men; and that the condition of the female sex decides the destiny of the nation," in her view a Christian nation. Hale's defense of woman's superiority was that it was only established through Christianity.

Hale believed that "her mind was honest in its search for truth," thereby claiming intellectual inquiry as a legitimate activity for women. Like Fuller, Hale did not imagine herself as "disempowered, but as a central figure in a quiet revolution to elevate the status of women even as she continued to validate their special role as moral arbiters." Yet, she did not support women's rights nor was she against slavery.

In another comprehensive study, similar to the one Hale had written in 1855, "Eminent Women of the Age, "Being; Narratives of the Lives and Deeds of the Most Prominent Women of the Present Generation" (1869), Hale had the intent to "develop and strengthen correct ideas respecting the influence of women, and their share in the privileges and responsibilities of human life." Authorities during that time frame, among them Horace Greeley, T. W. Higginson Abbott, Fanny Fern, and Elizabeth Cady Stanton, were asked to write sketches for the study.

Ellet also wrote a series of vignettes for Godey's recreated from other vignettes based on her books, *Women of the American Revolution,* in three volumes (1848-50) as well as collections of graphical sketches such as Pi*oneer Women of the West*. These performances were created onstage with female roles in a historical pageant that had always been presented from a masculine perspective.

Chapter 4

Affair of the Letters, A Fake Letter:
Poe, Osgood, Ellet

It was in 1846 that Ellet visited Poe's wife, Virginia Eliza Clemm Poe. Edgar and Virginia were first cousins and publicly married when she was 13 and he was 27. Virginia Poe shared Poe's letters to Osgood, and Ellet. Their contents presented cause for concern about Osgood's reputation. Maria Clemm also showed Ellet the letters on another occasion with other ladies present. After a visit with Virginia Poe, Ellet shared this information with other female writers in their group, including Ann Lynch Botta and Margaret Fuller. At the time Osgood was separated from her husband and Maria Clemm, Virginia Clemm's mother had told Ellet on a visit that Osgood was pregnant. Osgood ultimately requested her friends Margaret Fuller and Anne Lynch Botta retrieve her letters from Poe. The Poe Society characterizes this transaction entirely differently, saying that Ellet forced them to retrieve his letters. This resulted in a flurry of accusations from Poe attacking Ellet, saying he would return her letters to him. He referred to Ellet, Fuller and Botta as Osgood's "busy, bodies" and said Ellet should be concerned with her own letters. After the fact, being refused admittance at Lynch's soirees, Poe turned the tide with his Literati series in Godey's Lady's Book, giving positive commendations to Fuller and Osgood, while excluding Ellet, who he referred to as, "In person, short and much inclined to embonpoint." Translated plump, fleshy, referring to a bosom.

What was so disturbing in the Poe, Osgood letters that Ellet saw in 1846, other than two well-known literary figures, both married wooing via correspondences? In that era, it compromised both their reputations. Edward Wagenkneckt (1900- 2004) was a professor of English at Boston University, a major critic of and specialist on American literary authors, he believed that the Poe, Osgood relationship was not comprised of "clear distinctions, rather fact and fiction." Virginia's mother, Maria Clemm, who lived with Virginia and Edgar, initially showed the letters to Ellet, which precipitated Ellet's visit with Osgood, resulting in Margaret Fuller and Anne C.L. Botta's visit, both friends of Osgood, at her request. Fuller and Lynch also visited Poe to relinquish letters he was still in possession of, according to different historical renditions.

The conclusion by the Poe Society was that Ellet did this out of jealousy, her romantic interest in Poe was further insinuated in a letter the Poe Society publicized, which is in the Common Domain, that Ellet wrote Poe about the unfair removal of the President of the South Carolina College, where her husband, Dr. William Henry Ellet was professor. She requested that Poe include it in the Broadway Journal. Ellet wrote that she would write it, but she was concerned her husband would be "displeased." A much smaller detached note said, "call for it at her residence this evening," including a more a seductive phrase in German, though both were offered as one note. Through research and observation, the letter, which is two separate items, the smaller item inferring romantic interest is not written in Ellet's hand. The Poe behemoth ultimately added a disclaimer, which states that part of the letter, including the more forward intent of interest, written in German, was in fact written in another hand, other than Ellet's, though it had been previously offered by them as Ellet's romantic overture to Poe in a letter. It's nonsensical, that the letter Ellet wrote to Poe openly declaring her concern for her husband's feelings, would in that same letter declare her affections for Poe, which is what Poe claimed and the Poe et al kept defending after a century of libelous accusations focused on a long-deceased writer, who doesn't have a conglomerate, worth millions, defending her…

Other pertinent and missing information comes from "A Reexamination of a Poe Date: Mrs. Ellet's Letters," by James Reece. After Ellet asked Poe to produce her letters, he, fearing retaliation from Ellet's brother for not relinquishing them, (if there even was compromising letters) and asking Thomas Dunn English if he would be his second in a duel, also if English would loan him his pistol. The duel never took place, but On June 23, 1846 Poe sent an apology letter to Ellet. Where is that letter? Why haven't Poe et al produced it? What we do know is that Ellet's apology letter to Osgood, July 8, 1846 is in the Common Domain, accessible to all. And this letter claims that the letter Ellet saw at the Poe's house was a fake. Who might have created the letter? Maria Poe Clemm, Virginia Poe's mother? Maria inquired of Ellet if Osgood was still married and if she was pregnant! She showed the letters at tea parties and appears to be a conniving, self-interested, and unprincipled woman the more she is revealed through those who knew her.

In another attempt at misinformation by Poe's defenders, in what was and is a failure to reveal all the facts, by not citing Maria Poe Clemm's supposed concern for Poe and Osgood's relationship and her contact with Ellet to be in the know, so to speak, was not included by Poe defender Kelly Keener in *In Missing Letter Found: An Epistle Written by Frances Sargent Osgood to Elizabeth Ellet in Connection with the Poe-Osgood Scandal*. They refer to Ellet and Maria Clemm as Osgood's calumniators.

What remains today and is blatantly an appeal to resurrect Poe's dalliance with a married woman in an era when men were beyond reproach, but women were legally subordinate to men in every way, regardless, Osgood and Poe both became recipients of derision for their failure to publicly resolve their relationship status, while Ellet was demeaned for her concern for Osgood. Why it's more likely that Ellet was acting out of concern and not jealousy, her record of coming to the aid of women, writing solely about women in an age of male domination, having a marriage unsullied by unfaithful behavior, she was on more solid ground than Poe ever was reputationally. Yet, Keener posits that Ellet could do what she wanted since her husband was still in South Carolina. Now that's fantastically contrived.

"In Poe's Major Crisis" by Sidney P. Moss, he wrote how differently the events at Lynch's literary soirees would have ended after Poe's reading of the Raven, essentially saying, if only Poe wasn't Poe, if only Osgood wasn't Osgood, which would have avoided the so-called "malicious" Ellet. Poe would not have lashed out at everyone in "The Literati of New York City," nor become involved in a libel suit because of it. If only those who perpetrated falsehoods to disguise Poe's behavior, his penchant for retribution and womanizing, which ended his popularity, didn't evolve into his predicament in the first place. Context, it was Poe who was served with a Libel Suit. He was heavily in debt and was outed from the Literati. Having threatened to publish private communications, he became the recipient of attacks. Two New York papers wrote that Poe, "was at present in a state of health which renders him not completely accountable for all his peculiarities" because he had recently adopted an "extreme" solution to escape the so-called persecution of Mrs. Ellet. This identical script is repeated by Griswold when it came to Ellet and his divorce proceedings, which is not surprising, considering their competitive, complicated relationship.

Keener frames the Poe, Osgood dalliance and public access of a letter she undoubtedly came across in Ellet's Autograph Album, which the Poe Society purchased, "The purpose of this article is to place the content of this letter before the community of Poe scholars, and to further explore its relevance for Poe scholarship."

What the Poe, Osgood tryst relayed, concurrently with *The Raven,* at the height of Poe's popularity, is that the accuser's only recourse was to deflect and blame it on the accused. It's referred to as gaslighting, "redirecting or "deflecting" blame for *one's own mistake* onto someone else in an attempt to preserve one's own self-image.

Keener's assessment of Ellet supports the Poe conglomerate's position, using their attack lines, that Ellet was "meddlesome, thieving and vindicative." Is that scholarship of gossip? Fuller and Lynch, who retrieved the letters from Osgood were accused of being "busy buddies" by Poe. Why did Kelly Kenner, likely at the behest of the Poe Society, purchase Ellet's autograph album over one hundred and fifty years later? Separating out Poe's undeniable gifts and literary craft, while denying his immoral character, appears to be the ultimate goal of Poe defenders. Rather than scholarly, it's more like camouflage, concealment.

As to Ellet's letters, all females seeking Poe's attention, publication in the Broadway Journal, wrote him. It's well known that many female writers of that era were flirtatious in regard to seeking Poe's approval for publication in the Broadway Journal, for complimentary critiques and publication in Godey's Lady's Book, without intending explicit romantic interest. Poe wrote love letters to Sarah Helen Whitman, who was married. Where are those letters? Where are the Poe, Osgood letters? It doesn't take Sherlock Holmes to figure out Poe's 21st Century behemoth, making millions off of retreaded gossip is looking for more who-done-its.

As stated previously it was Virginia Poe's mother, Maria Poe Clemm, who appeared to be distraught by Poe's affair of the letters with Osgood, and it was Ellet's intent to give warning to Frances Sargent Osgood, which is the context missing in the Poe conglomerate's attacks on Ellet. Osgood's position was that Poe's wife, Virginia Clemm Poe, supported their relationship as someone who kept Poe abstinent and as a potential partner in the event she died. Was Ellet's interference due to her own romantic interest in Poe, it seems unlikely, because she was supported by other female writers in their literati group who viewed her intentions as altruistic and supportive. Ellet's proactive defense of women, demonstrated over and over again that helping women, was an example of her continued stance to protect, rather than being meddlesome.

Another factor missing, important context concerning their relationship, is that Virginia Poe, whose marriage to Edgar was more or less arranged by Maria Clemm, who had much more influence than has been revealed. Virginia was not well and it's unlikely that Poe and Virginia's marriage consisted of conjugal relations. She wasn't of legal age to marry, meaning those who certified the marriage committed perjury. Poe's defenders talk about Virginia as his one true love, which doesn't correlate with his womanizing. His penchant, his consistency in killing off his female characters as a reoccurring theme, writing love poems to other women, not just Osgood, while Virginia was still alive, doesn't jibe with Virginia being the love of his life.

In contrast, what I now know about Ellet, minus the Poe behemoth's 98-year-old history to implant their version of the 19th century into the 20th and 21 Century, is nothing less than Poe's tales reborn. You will never read on their pages that Ellet was more interested in coming to the aid of women in need, not just for charitable assistance, but in ways that at the time, Poe might not have known about or if he did, he wasn't going to divulge her involvement and deeds to help women from his most favored scapegoat. Out of all the ladies in their literary group and others seeking his approval and publication, not one of them spoke ill of Ellet. Many of them puffed editors and critiques for good reviews, including flirty overtures.

Ellet's consistent endeavors to address the inequities women faced to protect them against husbands who abused them, in one way or another, was not necessarily well-known at that time, as much of their communications were done via private letters, but certainly women's rights leaders, abolitionists knew, because Ellet was communicating and involved with them, including Elizabeth Cady Stanton, Feminist, Women's Rights Advocate, Lydia Mott, abolitionist, feminist, and Susan B. Anthony, Feminist, Woman's Rights Advocate, who wrote Ellet asking her to provide refuge for a woman and her child running away from an abusive husband. We know this by way of a footnote in edited papers of Stanton and Anthony asking for assistance in 1860 to conceal a woman and her daughter. There is no question Ellet's New York life revolved around America's most well-known women's rights advocates:

- *Ellet was involved in Elizabeth Cady Stanton's attempt to aid Elizabeth Packard and her child who sought refuge from her husband who had put her in an asylum.*
- *Ellet promoted charities for impoverished women and children by speaking in public to raise funds.*
- *Ellet wrote feminist, abolitionist Lydia Mott to locate a woman and man in 1861. Between 1861-65 New York was involved in the Civil War*
- *Ellet helped spiritualist Margaret (Maggie) Fox Kane with her financial situation, and through that association anonymously compiled the book, The Love Life of Dr Kane*
- *Ellet wrote Osgood about doing a book together from historic text that needed translations in which Ellet excelled.*
- *Ellet and Ann S. Stephens interceded on behalf of Griswold's wife in a divorce case involving his proposals to two women while married to Mrs. Charlotte Meyer Griswold, his second wife, while simultaneously romancing the poet, Alice Carey*
- *Griswold's wife, Charlotte Meyers Griswold and Ellet wrote letters to Alice Craig and Harriet McCrillis, who both expected a proposal of marriage to Griswold, while he was still married to Charlotte Meyers Griswold*
- *At the Request of Susan. B. Anthony Ellet and Abby Hopper Gibbons, an abolitionist, helped conceal Phoebe Harris Phelps, and her daughter in New York, and facilitated her journey to Scranton, PA., away from her abusive husband.*

The virulent condemnations against Ellet from the Poe conglomerate and Poe himself, accusations that Ellet was "jealous, petty, cruel and an instigator," and that all the women were "busy-bodies," is a demonstration of Poe's general demeanor, exemplifying a propensity to chastise strong, outspoken women, those who disagreed with him or uttered a word against him, not a Poe behavior entirely dissimilar from how he treated writers from New England, who Poe vehemently defiled over differences in their beliefs. They referred to Poe as the "hatchet-man" for his biting criticisms and accusations of plagiarism, and inadequacies of their writing style. Whether Poe was always an amiable gentleman depended on his audience. He was known to be generally opinionated, crass, egotistical and frequently imbibed in opiate and alcohol consumption which affected his demeanor, his mindset.

Nevertheless, considering more than 150 years of missing context, and I will repeat this throughout, while the Poe Society seeks a letter, they say is missing from June 19, 1846 that will further corroborate Ellet's insistence on prolonging the Poe Osgood scandal. Ironically, as mentioned before, Poe sent Ellet a letter of apology on June 23, 1846. Ellet sent Osgood a letter of apology, in July, 8, 1846, writing she would have sent it before. This is a letter claiming that the Poe, Osgood letter in contention was fake, which was news to me, despite all my research, a letter that has likely been in the common domain for a long time, has escaped public visibility entirely. The letter will be further explained in another chapter.

Poe, easily moved on from Osgood after her death with Sarah Helen Whitman, who represented everything Poe had loathed about the Bluestocking women of the New York Literati, Fuller, Ellet and others. Whitman supported feminism and spiritualism, and liberalism in her writing. Fascinating, because Ellet approached writing about women's roles, whether it was in the kitchen, as artists or defending our nation, rather than espousing isms of the day, she wrote about women's lives, and the separate spheres treatment they experienced, which was the only acceptable roll 19th century men abided by.

This is a letter Ellet sent to Osgood, who was ill with tuberculosis, which contradicts what has been repeated, that Ellet prolonged the Ellet-Osgood letter scandal, according to the Poe Society. *"Be assured I shall preserve utter silence in future on the subject... only saying... that you have been traduced, wrongfully."* Ellet continues, *"Most fervently do I hope you may soon forget the whole painful affair—that your health & spirits may return."*

The only part of Ellet's letter that was not included by Keener referenced the fake letter, though the entire letter was in the index.

What's important to note is that Ellet's response quoted by the Poe Society, above, is only one letter out of several Keener has made public, included in Kelly Keener's "In Missing Letter Found." Keener should ensure that the entirety of Ellet's autograph album is made public, because to use it piecemeal as a weapon, as demonstrated above, and by only sharing passages intended to continue to defame Ellet, is emblematic of a strategy to project blame in perpetuity.

In Missing Letter Found: An Epistle Written by Frances Sargent Osgood to Elizabeth Ellet in Connection with the Poe-Osgood Scandal, by Kelly Keener, two of Osgood's letters are reproduced bemoaning her illness and attributing her worsening malaise, likely death, due to Ellet. Osgood ends the letter with this statement, *"I think Mr. Poe should be forgiven for his part in the matter—as he confessed to me that he had intervals of madness. I have neither heard nor seen anything of him for months."*

What other reason would Keener have to purchase Ellet's autograph album, other than to try and corroborate Ellet's romantic interest in Poe, and perpetuate Poe's claim he had Ellet's letters? Which he admitted he did not. Why else would Keener purchase Ellet's autograph album? In view of the fact most female writers were doing what Hollywood actresses have been forced to do for decades, appeal to men who were in control of studios. In the 19th century women were not legally recognized to become writing professionals, and it was illegal for women to even perform professionally as actresses in Europe until the 17th century. Acting in the United States wasn't legal until the 1800s. What did women have to do to get Poe to consider their work for publication without putting out, so to speak, by sending flirtatious vibes.

Consider, Osgood, for instance, whom he favored, is a no-name today as far as her literary contributions are concerned. Whereas Fuller and Ellet are well known today for their contributions to literature, due to their feminist stance, which put them into an exclusive group of 19th Century feminist writers relating to an era of change when women strove for a voice, for independence. It has been stated that Poe puffed the worthiness of lesser female writers for monetary recompense, and as we know, he attacked Fuller and Ellet in particular, only because he disfavored Ellet and Fuller for what he deemed female intrusiveness and found them both unattractive. Unless they were writers he approved of, which excluded their moral, equitable, political positions, his protestations were intended to defame and discredit them. It's Fuller and Ellet who are read and admired today for their progressive insight into the roles of women and their plight for equal rights, not Poe, not Osgood.

Once Poe's editorial and publishing authority disappeared, so did the critiques, the publishing opportunities and the income, especially from female writers and certainly after the Osgood scandal. But his protestations against Ellet didn't end. It's not unsurprising that he was referred to by men as "tomahawk man" and "broad-axe man."

The continued attempts at vindication of Poe, by the Poe Society, as to his social behavior are akin to what we read today in tabloids and movie magazines featuring the gossip and accusations made by well-known people. Certainly, flirtation was in vogue during the 19th century era of flirtatious, "Saucy Escort" cards. Being that Osgood was well known as a "consummate flirt," it's not surprising that out of all the married women attending Lynch's literary soirees, it was Osgood who allured Poe to her clutches, for both literary achievement and a romantic dalliance.

Concerning the letter debacle, Thomas Dunn English claimed Ellet had never written inappropriate letters to Poe, despite Poe's accusations. Poe, who successfully sued English and the *New York Mirror* for libel pertaining to another matter in 1847, which still indicated the animosity between them. English's defense of Ellet certainly aggravated Poe. Dunn was a physician, Democrat statesman, editor, author, novelist, poet, and satirist. The Poe behemoth vehemently discredits Dunn's accounts, nevertheless the Poe, Osgood controversy put a damper on attendance at the soirees. It was in fact, Poe who was refused admittance at Lynch Botta's salons, not English nor any other male attendees. Horace Greeley, then editor of the *New York Daily Tribune*, said Poe had "scandalized two eminent literary ladies," referring to Osgood and Ellet.

English was an American physician, Democratic statesman, editor, author, novelist, poet and satirist and friend of Elizabeth Fries Ellet. English frequently defended her against Poe's accusations, even resulting in Poe having the temerity to ask him to be his second and provide him with a gun in a shoot-out with Ellet's brother, over the infamous letter debacle, which never happened.

Thomas Dunn English

English was a regular attendee at Ann Lynch Botta's literary soirees and a Democratic statesman, who understood the plight of female authors. As a friend of Elizabeth Fries Ellet, English frequently defended her against Poe's accusations. His observations of Osgood's behavior at "dear Lynchie's soirees in comparison to the other literary ladies is the tell all. Poe wrote the *Cask of Amontillado with* English in mind as a revenge story. Poe wrote "Hop Frog" similarly to attack Elizabeth Ellet. Crossing Poe ultimately resulted in bitter reprisals, ongoing in the 21st Century via Poe et al.

Thomas Dunn English

In A Reexamination of a Poe Date: Ellet's Letters, by James B. Reece, he included a snippet of *Reminiscences of Poe*, "Independent," 1896, comments by Thomas Dunn English, who clashed with Poe over the letters and was an American Democratic Party (which split due to slavery issues in 1860) politician from New Jersey. It should be noted that Poe himself, claimed that his statement that Ellet sent him inappropriate letters "was made during a seizure of madness," to avert a duel with Ellet's brother, Colonel William Lummis, according to the Poe et al, which is another of many renditions of what transpired in the overplayed, overdramatized affairs of the letters, with a decidedly never-ending fictious air.

English's comments about an evenings at one of Lynchie's soirees, as she was affectionately called, when Poe spoke, "So strongly was the scene impressed upon my memory that I can at any time close my eyes and... behold it in all its colors. In the plainly furnished room at one corner stands Miss Lynch with her round, cheery face, and Mrs. Ellet, decorous and ladylike, who had ceased their conversation when Poe broke into his lecture. On a sofa on the side of the room I sit with Miss Fuller, afterward the Countess Ossoli, on my right side, and Mrs. Elizabeth Oakes Smith on my left. At my feet little Mrs. Osgood, doing the infantile act, is seated on a footstool, her face upturned to Poe, as it had been previously to Miss Fuller and myself. In the center stands Poe, giving his opinions in a judicial tone and occasionally reciting passages with telling effect."

The recollections included in *A Reexamination of a Poe Date: Ellet's Letters,* by James B. Reece demonstrated the duality of opinions, rectifying Ellet's behavior in the matter, and affording a ring-side seat into what became an endless theatrical stage for the Poe conglomerate as evidenced here in a letter by Frances Sargent Osgood...

In Missing Letter Found, by author Kelly Keener, she includes a portion of Osgood's response to Ellet regarding the letter scandal. Ellet responded with an apology letter, which Keener writes about, but excludes the most pertinent sentences, even though the letter itself is at the end of the document. Ellet wrote that Osgood had been "grossly misrepresented and traduced," which means to expose to shame or blame by means of falsehood and misrepresentation. Ellet also wrote the letter was a forgery, which Keener also didn't include.

I am very ill—I had more to say—but I cannot write—May I beg of you, dear Mrs. Ellet, to let the matter drop here. I cannot live many months longer. I feel assured—but for my husband's sake & that of my children—I would not for the world have it revived—I do not wish the Poes ever to hear my name again— for I frankly own that I am afraid of such... me if you can—to the care of "Bartlett & Welford "Astor House" a line to assure me of your forgiveness—& believe [sic] me" I think Mr. Poe should be forgiven for his part in the matter—as he confessed to me that he had intervals of madness. I have neither heard nor seen anything of him for months. Yours sincerely F S Osgood. (no date)

Ellet wrote in response to Frances Sargent Osgood… *"The letter shown me by Mrs. Poe must have been a forgery, and man capable of offering to show notes he never possessed, would not, I think, hesitate at such a crime."*

Be assured I shall preserve utter silence in future on the subject... only saying... that you have been traduced, wrongfully." Ellet continues, *"Most fervently do I hope you may soon forget the whole painful affair—that your health & spirits may return.*

Mrs. Ellet's five-page letter includes a statement to Mrs. Frances S. Osgood dated July (7) 1846, apologizing for her part in the derogatory gossip which had circulated about Mrs. Osgood in connection with the affair, Ellet expressing regret that her explanation had not been made earlier. Mrs. Ellet wrote that "it was written months ago- but I feared you would not receive it in a candid spirit and therefore destroyed it." Reexamination of Poe Date, Mrs. Ellet's letters, by James B. Reece. But Reece doesn't mention that Ellet states the letter was a fake. Nor does Kelley Kenner in "Missing Letter Found." But after Keener's source list, the letter Ellet wrote Osgood in response is now in the common domain in full, containing the statement that the letter was a forgery.

The longer five-page Ellet apology letter to Osgood in the Common Domain from which Reece provides a snippet that was written July (7) 8, 1846 and states:

I have this moment arrived in the city and received your letter dated June 19th, (the reason she did not get right back to Osgood), and deeply has it worried my heart in convincing me how poorly you have been misrepresented and traduced...the letter shown by Mrs. Poe must have been a forgery..." These snippets by Reece do not include Ellet's statement that the letter Ellet was shown by both Maria Clemm and Virginia Poe were forgeries.

Reexamination of Poe Date, Mrs. Ellet's letters, by James B. Reece wrote that, *"Mrs. Ellet sent a letter to Mrs. Osgood in July (1846) that neither had "anything to ap- prehend from the verbal calumnies of a wretch so steeped in infamy as he [Poe]." Keener did not include this portion in "Missing Letter Found."*

In a Reexamination of Poe Date, Mrs. Ellet's letters by James B. Reece, he writes about what transpired, which doesn't corroborate with Keener.

Mrs. Osgood denies sending him (Poe) an indiscreet letter. Although the surviving fragments of what was originally a longer letter by Osgood to Ellet do not feature such a denial, what text remains seems to be in accordance with Ellet's July 8 reply. It seems safe to conclude that these letter fragments do indeed date to June 19, 1846. Osgood says, one suspects with deliberate exaggeration, "May I beg of you, dear Mrs. Ellet, to let the matter drop here. I cannot live many months longer." Both Keener and Reece quote Osgood's statement.

Ellet's response, *"Be assured I shall preserve utter silence in future on the subject... only saying... that you have been traduced, wrong-*

fully." Ellet continues, *"Most fervently do I hope you may soon forget the whole painful affair—that your health & spirits may return."*

Reece writes the *"fragmentary Osgood letter is a strong contender for the missing June 19, 1846, (which Keener has said that there's a missing letter from that date) and is a link that not only displays Osgood's frazzled mental state, but it suggests Ellet persisted well after the fact."* Correction, in fact, in her last letter Ellet stated she would have *"sent it before, but she had just arrived back in the city,"* and was worried about Osgood's reaction, *"it was written months ago-but I feared you would not receive it in a candid spirit and therefore destroyed it,"* Ellet wrote. Another important missing element of Ellet's letter, now in the Common Domaine for all to see.

Time Table

- *Poe Osgood Literary Courtship began in 1845*
- *Ellet disclosed letters between Osgood and Poe Jan 1846*
- *Lynch removed Poe for Literary Soirees Early 1846*
- *Poe asked English to help with the Duel, which never happened June-23-1846*
- *Poe and Osgood met in 1845*
- *Fanny Faye Born June 1846*
- *Sam Osgood said he would sue Ellet 7-18-46*
- *Ellet apology letters to Osgood May/June/July 1846*
- *Ellet Refers to a Fake Letter July 8, 1846 letter*

Context on the letters from Pulitzer Prize Winner, Author Kenneth Silverman, who wrote in *Edgar A. Poe, A Biography, Mournful And Never-Ending Remembrance*, discussed by Rosenheim, Shawn in Review of *Never-Ending Biography*, by Kenneth Silverman and by Ljungquist, Kent J. Review of *Memory and Mourning*, by Kenneth Silverman. *Poe Studies/Dark Romanticism*, with a completely different assessment of the letter debacle. Silverman wrote, essentially one had to be sharp in Ellet's presence, meaning she was no pushover, which Poe discovered, giving him every cause to denounce her. Probably in January, she visited Poe at his Amity Street lodgings and saw a letter sent to him by Fanny Osgood. Again, the events are known through later and conflicting, and mostly second-hand accounts. What follows, is what we've heard from Poe and Poe et al ad nauseum. But Silverman wrote that "Poe's account was probably a lie." In July 1846, Osgood's husband, Samuel, demanded Ellet apologize to his wife, lest he sue her for defamation. Ellet responded in a letter, retracted her statements, and put the blame on Poe and his wife Virginia.

In the letter to Frances Osgood July 7/8, 1846, Ellet wrote that Osgood has been "grossly misrepresented." The letter shown to Mrs. Ellet by Mrs. Poe must have been a forgery. Ellet retracts the charges about Mrs. Osgood's relations with Poe, and "regrets her acquaintance with such people as the Poes."

This letter is in the common domain and context surrounding the letter will be explained, including what we didn't know about Maria Clemm, Virgina Clemm Poe's mother and her self-serving motives related to the Poe, Osgood relationship and the letters in question.

Here is an example of the literary ladies, not in support of Poe. Lynch was one of the ladies who retrieved the letters. Ellet's concern over Poe's letters, which indicated an ongoing romantic dalliance with Frances Sargent Osgood, resulted in swift retaliation. Osgood was married but separated. Poe continued to discredit Ellet's work and The Poe et al still supports his accusations against Ellet. *"Miss Lynch, who, according to Mrs. Elizabeth Oakes Smith, "was strict in drawing the moral as well as the intellectual line," " wrote after Poe's death, in an apparent allusion to Mrs. Ellet, that she had seen little of Poe in his last years "in consequence of a wide difference of opinion between us in reference to his treatment of another lady."*

Despite Poe's 19th century misogyny and frequent love entanglements and his romantic tryst with poet Frances Sargent Osgood, Ellet's intentions were not vindictive nor a jealous response, only a response to protect Poe's wife and Mrs. Osgood's reputation. It was also Virginia Poe's mother, Maria Poe Clemm, who appeared concerned about the letters and spoke of them when Mrs. Ellet visited the Poe house. The Poe conglomerate says Poe's wife, Virginia Poe, encouraged Osgood's relationship with Poe, as someone who could take her place. That may be true, but both were married at the time, though Osgood and her husband were separated in 1845.

Keener wrote that "Osgood was living with her husband and children in Philadelphia from early November 1846 through mid-March 1847." But the source she quoted was more specific in qualifying that "letters and writings confirm that Osgood was in Philadelphia "at least intermittently between November 1846 and March 1847."

In *"Read Here Thy Name Concealed": Frances Osgood's Poems on Parting with Edgar Allan Poe*, Mary De Jong writes that Osgood reunited with her husband, while she was still keeping tabs on Poe's life and interactions. Osgood's elegy, *The Hand that swept the sounding lyre,* was a tribute to Poe. Griswold's 1850 memoir of Poe contains statements Osgood made referring to Poe's marriage and his "many little poetical episodes," defining his interactions with other women, "with women other than his wife." Though this is likely true, Griswold is certainly not the most honest arbiter.

Mary De Jong wrote that it wasn't clear that Osgood's personal respectability was only questioned by Ellet and by Poe's mother-in-law, Maria Poe Clemm, who presents another facet in an ongoing reveal of possible motives from Maria to interfere in the Poe, Osgood relationship. What has also not been revealed by the Poe Society and Keener, is that scandalous stories about Osgood and Poe's dalliance spread widely beyond literary circles, even at that time and so did Ellet's victimization. All these years later, the Poe Society has made clear, demeaning Ellet to vindicate Poe is ongoing, while soliciting donations.

Anne Lynch Botta's New York Literary Soirées

Anne Lynch Botta

Anne Lynch Botta

Hostess of New York's Literary soirees, "Lynchie" as she was affectionately called by her attendees, is said to have had high moral character, her reasoning for forbidding Poe from attending after the Osgood affair and attacks against Ellet. Lynch Botta and

Margaret Fuller both went to retrieve the letters deemed harmful to Osgood's reputation.

As mentioned before, another factoid of lesser importance to the Poe Society, is that Anne Lynch Botta, careful of her own social respectability, avoided Poe and cautioned Whitman about being associated with him publicly. Lynch invited Osgood and Ellet to her Valentine's party in 1846, both attended. Poe was not invited, but he sent his Valentine's Day poem anonymously to Lynch's party at 116 Waverly Place in New York.

It was evident that despite the acrimonious air, Osgood had "devoted friends of both sexes." Inferring that her romantic liaison with Poe and public knowledge of the letters, its effect on their reputations and the ensuing defamation of Ellet, had not deterred Ellet nor Osgood from attending the same event, which suggests no acrimony between them.

William Gilmore Simms of Charleston, South Carolina, novelist and historian, who Ellet sought out for historical sources for "The Women of the American Revolution," asked Evert A. Duyckinck for more information about "Poe and the Ladies." The gossip was circulating, and Poe showed no interest in controlling it, even though Poe later admitted he didn't have letters from Ellet implying romantic interest, he still continued to defame and retaliate against Ellet. Poe's Literati sketches" in Godey's Lady's Book were published from May to October of 1846. In the final installment of Poe's Literati sketches in October 1846, Poe eliminated Ellet. Hiram Fuller's New York Evening Mirror sniped, "In scanning the verses of Mrs. Osgood [Poe] is quite at home," insinuating that the two were overly familiar.

In "Poe's Major Crisis" by Moss, William Gilmore Simms advice to Poe was to essentially to be a good husband and don't allow your desires to result in retaliation against those who fault you for an unbecoming show of faithlessness. It's even suggested by Moss, that Ellet coerced Fuller and Lynch to retrieve the letters because of her jealousy over the Poe Osgood tryst. It's difficult to find a redemptive or accurate word about Ellet in Moss. Also, it was Osgood who asked

Fuller and Lynch directly to retrieve the letters, which varies according to which account has been passed down.

The most nonsensical charade of the letters emanates from Poe's assertion he made a package of the letters and left it at Ellet's door. Ellet's response, which was deemed "meddlesome and hypocritical" by Poe's mostly male defenders, was to have her brothers prove that Poe had compromising letters from her. To that ultimatum, Poe response was that he had a fit of insanity. No matter what Ellet did or didn't do, she was the antagonist in Poe's separate spheres, misogynistic reality. His defenders, accusing her of forcing Fuller and Botta to retrieve the letters out of jealousy, is the most ludicrous, atypical line of defense, especially since Poe admitted he said he had her letters in a moment of madness. Which tale to believe when these insinuations run totally counter to Ellet's actions in protecting women from men like Poe and Griswold? Ellet's assistance to women may not have been known, or ignored by those who attacked her the most for being assertive in her dealings with self-adulating literary men, but much of it is documented now. Whether it was known at the time, her defamers were more likely to keep her actions unknown.

In Reexamination of a Poe Date: Mrs. Ellet's Letters, by James B. Reece, he writes of Poe's virtual banishment from Lynch's soirees of New York writers, where he had been a guest since the publication of *The Raven* a year earlier. Mrs. Ellet's wrote a letter to Osgood, dated July 8 (1846), apologizing for her part in the gossip which had circulated about the affair of the letters. It was then that Virginia Poe expressed a desire to move away from the city, to be removed from the gossip, which didn't fit with her approval of the Osgood, Poe dalliance as beneficial to Poe after her death. There exists an illogical variance between handing over the letters to Fuller and Lynch, and Virginia concerned about their liability and wanting to be removed from the gossip while Virginia was desirous of the Poe, Osgood romance extending beyond her death. Did Virginia know the letters were fake? How little she knew him, because he pursued another old dalliance with Sarah Helen Whitman, when Osgood was no longer in the picture, both Virginia Poe and Osgood dying before Poe died.

Ellet's motivation to ensure Osgood's letters were returned was deemed an act of jealousy or retribution as Poe asserted, rather it was an act of safeguarding her reputation, in consideration that Ellet and Ann S. Stephens were also involved in a Rufus Griswold divorce case, siding with Griswold's second wife Charlotte Meyer Griswold, while Griswold was attempting bigamy, by pledging marriage proposals to two other women and a romantic interest in the Poet Alice Cary.

In consideration that Ellet came to the aide of Margaret Kane Fox, compiling the love letters of Dr. Elisha Kane in the book, *The Love Life of Dr. Kane*, and giving credit to him for his love of Margaret, considering that and many instances of Ellet being a defender of women, Ellet's purported jealous motivations over letters between Poe and Osgood seem much less certain when viewed through a lens refined by over 150 years of perspective. Regardless, Poe's champions are still committed to defaming and discrediting Ellet. It comes across like the tabloids of today, depending on their particular loyalty, perpetuating story lines to sustain a preferred position, about a person, persons and their relationships.

In The Model Editions Partnership Historical Editions in the Digital Age, *The Papers of Elizabeth Cady Stanton and Susan B. Anthony,* we learn Ellet and Abby Hopper Gibbons, an abolitionist, school teacher and social welfare activist were involved in concealing Phoebe Harris Phelps and her daughter in New York, until they moved on to Philadelphia with assistance from Ellet. Phoebe, the wife of Charles Abner Phelps, suffered horrible domestic abuse. Over one hundred and fifty years later, Poe et al mentions Ellet's charitable contributions, but nothing about her involvement in assisting women who were abused, disenfranchised because of their beliefs, sent to asylums nor why they would purchase Ellet's autograph album other than for the purpose of the continuance of their legacy of fictional abuse and harm that further defaming her entails.

Ellet's autograph album was purchased anonymously in 2015, this information initially was aired by a Poe Society contributor Kelly Keener. Four years later Kelly Keener purchased Ellet's Autograph Album in 2019 for the Poe Society, likely with the intent of uncovering the hypothetical, love interest letters Ellet is accused of sending Poe. Osgood's letters and Elizabeth Ellet's autograph album are currently in the collection of Kelly Keener, which was purchased anonymously at first and later privately sold to Keener.

To further the Poe behemoth's attacks against Ellet over 150 years later, they've perpetuated Poe as the victim, Ellet as the villain. As in Montresor's Revenge in the "Cask of Amontillado," Poe is scapegoating Ellet, by declaring she penned romantic letters to him, while ultimately admitting there were none. For what other reason would the Poe et al have purchased her autograph album, via Kenner? No member of the Literati Ladies cited Ellet for inappropriate behavior, nor did the men, other than Griswold. The only man who would have agreed, who also had a romantic interest in Osgood and was furious over Ellet's and Stephen's defense of his second wife and marriage proposals to two other women simultaneously. Details on the divorce are in a law suit, which was essentially bigamy involving two other women, which is discussed further in Chapter Eight.

Sandra L. Langer, in *Women Artists in All Ages and Countries*, wrote that Mr. and Mrs. Ellet came back to New York together in 1848, (1849 is the date in the Duycinick Family Papers, NYPL) the romantic tryst between Osgood and Poe likely began in 1845-6, but *In Missing Letter found*, by Kelly Kenner, she wrote that "Ellet's husband was in South Carolina still teaching chemistry at the time, which gave Ellet the freedom to relay more than her thanks, but her romantic interest in Poe for featuring her work in the Broadway Journal." The problem with that statement is that it's likely that Henry and Elizabeth traveled back and forth during those years, as Henry was seeking another position in New York, before his final move. Mr. Ellet moved back to New York with his wife Elizabeth in 1849 because of his wife's wishes for him to sell their house and find work in New York. This is verified in the Evert Duyckinck Family Papers in the New York Public Library, and a letter from the South Carolina College, which is in chapter two.

Kenner relays that many would consider Ellet "meddlesome, thieving and vindictive." Not so, none of the ladies in the Literati group inferred any inappropriate behavior could be accrued to Ellet. Poe wrote in a letter to Annie Richmond in 1849, "I scorned Mrs. Ellet, simply because she revolted me," which appears to indicate his dislike for Ellet, just in terms of her physical appearance and obviously she did not fit the 19th century female stereotype of subservience, docility and coquetry. Ellet was not a flirt, Frances Osgood was. It's not as if Ellet was auditioning in a role dependent on her physical appearance. In film industry terms, we could compare Poe to Hollywood directors who for decades rarely made women's stories the focus of their films, but many of them certainly sexualized women.

Keener wrote that Virginia Poe, who knew of her illness, had in mind to support the ongoing relationship between Poe and Osgood, which was about much more than just letter exchanges, there were public, social meetings, dinners, theater, and trips. As to whether there were inappropriate letters from Ellet to Poe, that has never been re-solved depending on who you ask, but it's why Keener purchased El-let's Autograph Album on behalf of the Poe et al. Keener wrote that Poe, Osgood and Ellet were disgraced, but it was Poe, not Osgood, not Ellet, that was refused admittance. Only Poe's behavior was reviled, thus his presence was forbidden. Keener also inferred that Ellet perpet-uated the attacks which would seem unlikely since Ellet wrote a letter to Osgood about doing a book together from historic text that needed translations, which Ellet excelled at, does this relay a persistence in defaming Osgood? Though we don't know the exact date of the let-ter, it's certainly within the time frame of the Literati soirees they all attended.

A Fake Letter

Time Line

- *Maria Clemm, Virginia's mother shows Ellet and Other Women the letter(s) in Question at a Tea Party at their home*
- *Osgood refers to Maria Clemm and Ellet as collaborators against her*
- *Ellet is shown letters by both Maria Clemm and Virginia Poe in visits with them*
- *Margaret Fuller and Anne Botta Lynch go to retrieve the letter(s)*
- *Poe defends himself, accuses Ellet of writing him letters, said he returned them, then challenged by Ellet's brothers to show them, Poe claims insanity*
- *Samuel Osgood threatens Ellet with a law suit*
- *Ellet declares the letter(s) a fake in a four-page letter to Osgood July-(7)8-1846*

Another significant twist is the fake letter in question, which is in the common domain and accessible to all, which was transcribed by Keener in "Missing Letter Found" and included in between two lists of sources at the end of her document, rather than in the body of her article. It's a letter Ellet wrote to Osgood July (7) 8, 1846, in which Ellet wrote, *"Mrs. Osgood has been grossly misrepresented." The Letter shown to Mrs. Ellet by Mrs. Poe must have been a forgery. Ellet retracts her charges about Mrs. Osgood's relations with Poe and regrets her acquaintance with such people as the Poes."*

Ellet explains that the compromising letter in question, involving Poe and Osgood's romantic dalliance was a fake, this after Osgood's husband threatened to sue Ellet, in which she wrote that Osgood had "been grossly misrepresented." The letter shown to Mrs. Ellet initially by Maria Clemm, Virginia Poe's mother, was likely shown again to

Ellet by Virginia Poe. Ellet retracted her charges in regard to the letter, and her regrets as to knowing the Poes in the four-page letter to Osgood, after being threatened by Samuel Osgood. The Poe Society and its defenders have deflected any culpability for his romantic entanglement by putting blame on Ellet. Both Fuller and Lynch saw the letter, so it's incomprehensible, but when you follow the entire Poe charade, it appears everyone was misled, but by who? Why didn't the Poe Society produce Ellet's letters to Poe or the Poe letter to Osgood in question, which Ellet said was a fake, could it be because they knew it was a fake, that it would be so incriminating as to cause another scandal?

There has been no mention that it was Osgood who appealed to Fuller and Lynch in much of what has been available to the public, other than from Kenneth Silverman's *"Edgar A. Poe, A Biography, Mournful And Ever Ending Remembrance,"* evidently Ellet understood how Poe dealt with adversity and truth and what she referred to as that "fearful paragraph" Virginia Poe read to her, must have been forged. What was in that fearful paragraph? We don't know, because those letters, which could have been destroyed by Maria Clemm, more on this in the next chapter, or that Poe et al have never divulged its contents and made it available to the public.

In Kenneth Silverman's book, another door opens to truths related to Poe and Ellet. Silverman wrote that Poe turned his attentions away from Osgood and became interested in Ellet in 1845. This interest led to Poe featuring Ellet's work in his soon to expire *Broadway Journal*. Poe referred to Ellet as one of the most accomplished writers of her era. In that timeframe, he only published Osgood in the starring position once. Poe reached out to Duyckinck for other favors related to Ellet. The only explanation of Poe's attention focused on Ellet, according to Silverman, is that she may have been more accessible. Osgood was aware of this and didn't hide her covetous, envious side.

Silverman referred to Ellet as a "formidable, and knowledgeable woman." In all, Silverman makes the point there are so many conflicting renditions of these times, and after a few years, Poe remarked that he wouldn't blame Ellet if she referred to him as a "cad." Silverman praised Ellet's translations, her multi-volume work, Women of the American Revolution and as the first white female on a dangerous trip to Lake Minnetonka, in Minnesota. Not unsurprisingly, Keener is not keen on Silverman's rendition of Ellet, Poe and Osgood.

We still don't know the contents of the letters in question and until we do, only Ellet and Osgood's letters, not Poe's, are public. The mystery of those letters has not been resolved, while Poe et al have only been on the hunt for Elizabeth Fries Ellet's letters, letters he admitted she never wrote. How does that fit into Poe's *Tales, Mysteries and Contrivances*? What we do know via Silverman is Poe's account of the letters was likely a lie. Through Thomas Dunn English's accounts, the events are totally dissimilar from Poe's. English wrote that Ellet had not written letters to Poe. Even after fisticuffs between Ellet's brother and Poe, in which Poe walked away saying he gave English a flogging, which may or may not be true.

Flagrant deception and disregard for historical evidence and testimony refutes any truthful accounting by Poe devotees perpetuating a false narrative by eliminating historical evidence, which is not scholarship. Poe himself said there were no letters from Ellet in contention, not once, but on many occasions in response to what had become an ongoing intrusion into both their lives. Also, Poe's penitent for hoaxes or his romantic interest in Ellet indicated by Pulitzer Prize winner Kenneth Silverman in his book *Edgar A. Poe A Biography, Mournful and Never-Ending Remembrance*. Did Ellet rebuff Poe's attention in those early stages of their association? Ellet is being accused of destroying letters, which is not a historical verifiable fact, but it has been verified that letters were destroyed by Poe's mother-in-law Maria Clemm Poe, likely including Poe's letters and other correspondences.

You would think that the Poe et al, and their volunteers who meticulously save every correspondence related to Poe would have some of the letters in question in their possession. Also, there is no statement, other than from Kelly Keener, who initially purchased Ellet's autograph album, which is now owned by the Poe conglomerate, an autograph album over 150 years old, which contained letters that they hoped would vindicate and verify their continued attacks against Ellet. This disregard for historical evidence and testimony discounts the Poe defenders' accounting of the letters because Poe himself denied Ellet sent him letters of romantic nature, many times, no mention of that and no mention by the Poe volunteers that Ellet's apology letter saying that Poe's letters in question were fake, likely at the hand of Maria Clemm Poe who disapproved of Poe's relationship with Osgood. And the fragment in German inferring Ellet's romantic interest in Poe by the Poe Society, was much later referred to as a fragment that was not written in Ellet's hand.

Letters which are still widely unknown, is that famed women's rights activists Elizabeth Cady Stanton and Susan B. Anthony corresponded with Ellet. Anthony contacted Ellet in 1860, asking her to give asylum to a woman and her daughter fleeing her abusive husband in New York. Ellet helped conceal them both, and Anthony wrote of the sensationalized case in a letter to Stanton. There were many women who would have fit that need, including Elizabeth Packard, a social reformer who was locked in an insane asylum, and sought a safe haven from her husband. She had connections with Susan B. Anthony and Lydia Mott. It's likely that Ellet may have given refuge to Mrs. Packard, unknowing to the public. In another case, Ellet gave refuge to Mrs. Phoebe Harris Phelps, children's book author fleeing her abusive husband, with her child. Ellet arranged passage on a train to Philadelphia for Harris Phelps. With the perspective of time, it's unlikely that Poe or anyone of his supporters were aware of Ellet's involvement that would not have been publicly aired to protect Phelps, her child and other women in dire circumstances. Ellet helped arrange a trip with the Office of the New York Express in a letter dated 6-21-1851, without mentioning Harris Phelps name.

What we know about Ellet's contributions, by way of a footnote in the edited papers of Stanton and Susan B. Anthony, is that Anthony herself turned to Ellet for assistance often. What this indicates is that Ellet was known by the most prominent American women's rights advocates because of her record to coming to the aid of women, but seldom were these alliances known publicly, since much of these transactions were done privately via letters. Perhaps this was partially due to the fact, Ellet didn't want to alienate her broader audience, including that of Godey's Lady's Book, and its publisher Sarah Josepha Hale whose audience was mixed, both separate spheres, leaning more toward the cult of true woman hood and to protect the women involved in fleeing abuse.

As a member of New York's Literary Society which included poet greats like Henry Wordsworth Longfellow, William Cullen Bryant and accomplished women writers, Margaret Fuller, Anne S. Stephens, Elizabeth Fries Ellet and the poet Frances Sargent Osgood, Louisa May Alcott and many others, they all attended literary soirees, which were held weekly at the home of poet Anne Charlotte Lynch Botta, referred to by her guests as "my dear Lynchie."

Poe's popularity after "The Raven" brought many letters soliciting praise and visitors, including Ellet, who on a visit to his home, his wife Virginia Poe showed Ellet letters from Osgood to Poe, which Ellet deemed compromising to Mrs. Osgood. Which is now perceived as a fake letter. The question today, is, where are Poe and Osgood's letters to each other? Why is the Poe Society only concerned with Ellet's letters? Which on its face, begs the question, what are they hiding?

Ellet, Poe, Rufus Griswold, and other well-known writers, editors and critics frequented the New York Literati Group's soirees held by Anne C. Lynch Botta, attended by many female writers including Ann S. Stephens, an American novelist and magazine editor, author of dime novels and credited as the originator of that genre, Frances Sargent Osgood, poet and love interest of Poe, Margaret Fuller, an American journalist, editor, critic, translator and, Elizabeth Fries Ellet, the first women to write about women's participation in *The Women of the American* Revolution 1, 11, 11 and other Bluestocking women, educated, with intellectual and literary interests, as well as well-known male writers of that era including William Makepeace Thackeray, William Cullen Bryant, Ralph Waldo Emerson, Herman Melville, Oscar Wilde, Horace Greeley, Thomas Dunn English, Cassius Clay, politician and anti-slavery crusader and others.

Fake Letter, Maria Clemm Poe, "Motherly, Dastardly"

Ann S. Stephens verified that Poe's wife Virginia Eliza Clemm Poe showed Ellet incriminating letters from Osgood to Poe on a visit with her. With the permission of Osgood, both Margaret Fuller and Anne C. Lynch Botta visited Virginia Poe to retrieve the letters that they deemed had the potential to ruin her reputation. There are many confusing renditions on Fuller and Lynch's visits to retrieve the letters in question, as are the stories associated with the letter scandal. Nevertheless, the result was Poe was ostracized and he blamed Ellet for what he defined as gossip and excluded her from a series he did on writers in their literary circle in *Godey's Lady's Book.* Context, the letters Maria Clemm and Mrs. Virginia Poe showed Ellet were deemed fake by Ellet, in a letter to Osgood dated July (7) 8, 1846.

Another question that remains, if Osgood had deemed the letters were not compromising, why not have a discussion with Fuller and Botta and refuse to release the letters to them, and where are those letters now? It's a fair assumption that by giving the letters to Fuller and Botta, Osgood was admitting the concern she had for her reputation, which doesn't match with the sentiments from Poe that he was behaving appropriately, nor the revelation by Ellet, that the letters were fake. The only rational conclusion is that Poe et al, preferred that the letters remained private, until the fake letter showed up in Keener's "Missing Letter Found," without referring to it as a fake letter in here response, but including the letter as a source only. Over 150 years later, the deceptive letter or letters, are still earning fallout, and could be Poe and the Poe conglomerate's most successful con job and or it could be the act of a cunning mother-in-law to cover up her own misdeeds! To hypothesize that Ellet backed down for fear of a lawsuit, seems much less plausible, since Maria Clemm invited women to tea to show them letters, including Ellet. What's nonsensical, albeit not out of the realm of possibility, is that Maria Clemm concocted the contents of the letters in question.

We know so little about Virginia, other than her marriage to Poe was an arrangement, atypical in that era and that her mother, Maria Clemm hoped that relationship could ensure a livelihood for her and Virginia, who had wasting disease. Virginia, who Poe referred to as "Sis" was 13 and Poe, 27. Certainly not unremarkable to believe they never consummated their marriage.

"In Maria Clemm, Poe's Aunt: His Boon or His Bane," by Burton A. Pollin, in recollections by John H. Ingram, an English biographer and editor of Poe, who had collected documents related to the Poe family. This led Ingram to discoveries about Mrs. Clemm, which identified her solicitous nature. An example of her avarice and dishonesty is that after seeing Poe's obits in a local paper, Maria contacted a Poe friend requesting that he ask Griswold to visit her for a message from Edgar.

The message was a collection of Poe's publications that were "conceived" by Maria and Stella Lewis, with edited or revised copies of his works that Poe left with Maria. With the editing process and publication, Maria added "legal and publication rights to Griswold." But this was all a scheme to gain recompense for both, and lodgings for Maria, which invariably failed to produce the monetary stability Maria desired.

John Carl Miller who wrote "Building Poe Biography" cited "Maria's jealousy and destruction of many preserved letters from Poe's female friends, some of great fame." Where then are Osgood's and Ellet's letters? The Poe researcher, Thomas Mabbot, described Maria as "domineering, tergiversating, mendacious, meddlesome, insincere, hypocritical, self-serving and profoundly untrustworthy."

There are five pages in the letter Ellet wrote Osgood in July of 1846 and in "Missing Letter Found, an Epistle by Frances Sargent

Osgood," author Kelly Keener, who quoted Ellet, who wrote "Osgood had been traduced." What was not included by Keener is the details that the letter Ellet was first showed to her by Maria Clemm at one of her tea parties, where other women also saw the letter, and the letter Virginia Poe showed her were ultimately deemed a fake by Ellet. The fact Keener excluded that mention, choosing not to use it to incriminate Ellet is very telling. Also, Keener wrote that Osgood asked her dear friends Fuller and Lynch to pick up the letters, which has been has consistently attributed to Ellet by the Poe defenders. In John Carl Miller's "Building Poe's Biography," he wrote that Maria had trashed many of Poe's letters from well-known literary people after his death.

In Terence Martin's, "The Imagination at Play," Edgar Allen Poe, he writes that "hoaxes, puzzles, puns and jokes abound in Poe's work..." also, he repeatedly used themes that invert reality and that "Poe is not above playing a trick on the reader." Here's a talent Poe didn't only utilize on fiction, writing about the horror of cannibalism in "The Narrative of Aurthur Gordon Pym of Nantucket," he was said to have "sandbagged his audience by reverting to normalcy, leaving the reader totally uncertain about what took place." What a trick to employ in diffusing a romantic liaison, creating a fake love letter and incriminating Ellet by setting her up.

Regardless of whether the letter Maria Clemm and Virginia Poe showed Ellet was fake or not, Poe's romantic tryst with poet Frances Osgood, while married to Eliza Clemm Poe, was still the downfall of his popularity among women of the Literary soirees. Was this fake letter alone, which Ann Lynch Botta retrieved, enough to stop inviting him or was it also his and Osgood's conduct which verified their romantic tryst? After the soiree invites stopped, Poe then proceeded to retaliate by eliminating Ellet from his Literati publication in Lady's Godey's book. Poe implied it was Ellet who wrote Osgood's letters, which sounds more and more atypical of his penchant for making up lies about people he hated. Ellet asserted that the letters were fake. Poe suggested Ellet should come to pick up her letters to him, letters that have never been found, which Poe later said did not exist, all which resembles a Poe-like plot from one of his own fictitious stories, similar to ones in current love triangles we see in movies and books. Whodunit plots! Can anyone disagree that Poe, whose revenge seeking, both real and fictional, was a driving force in his life and in his fantasy driven imagination, replete with intricately gleaned plots, scapegoats, like the ones derived in the *Cask of Amontillado*? Poe wrote, "the narrator seeks revenge on Fortunato because he mortally insulted him." Poe's revenge against Ellet turned her into a spectacle of literary horror in *Hop-Frog, a* denunciation of Ellet and the Bluestocking ladies who supported her. Ultimately could Poe have set Ellet up, since his loathing of her was apparent and important enough for the Poe behemoth to perpetuate these accusations over 150 years later?

All the women writers in the New York Literary Group communicated with each other and with Poe through letters, many of which were requests for publication and invitations. Many were likely enamored with him and or puffed his interest in their writing with overt flirting. Ellet wrote and interacted with Poe, as did all the ladies desirous of receiving favorable critiques, yet there was no controversy that erupted from Ellet's husband, chemist William Henry Ellet who traveled back and forth, as did Ellet from South Carolina to New York and Dr Ellet moved back to New York permanently in 1849, likely in conjunction with selling the house there and eventually working for the Manhattan Gas Company in 1852. Dr. Ellet could have been in New York at the time of the showdown between Poe and Ellet.

There was no concurrence from other female writers in the group that Ellet's letters to Poe were in question. Regardless, Poe's letters had the potential to harm Frances Osgood's reputation and his as well as casting a shadow on Ellet. But it was Poe who was shunned by the women in the New York Literary group, according to every source. It was Poe who no longer was invited to weekly soirees, and his response was to write critiques of the New York's Literary Society for the *Godey's Lady's Book* in 1846, eliminating Ellet. He was complimentary of Fuller and Osgood, particularly Frances Sargent Osgood whom he had exchanged letters of a romantic nature; but he excluded Ellet, who bore the brunt of what was essentially Poe's own acts of indiscretion. Was it based on Ellet's concern or jealousy? Being that Virginia Poe's mother Maria Clemm showed Ellet the letters initially, whose concerns, dubious though they may have been, nevertheless it alerted Ellet and were relevant in understanding what Maria's true motives were. Intriguing that Kelly Kenner referred to Maria Clemm and Ellet as Poe detractors! Now that we know Ellet deemed the letter a fake, who wrote it or altered the Poe letter in question and why? Was it Maria Clemm or a Poe hoax?

Ellet's letter to Francis Sargent Osgood apologizing and explaining that the letter Ellet was shown was a fake is in the public domain, why then isn't the Poe Society glomming on to the most important aspect, that Maria Clemm and Virginia Poe showed Ellet a fake letter, which resulted in Ellet's profusive four-page apology? Would the brutally frank and benevolent Ellet, who helped numerous women escape from dire situations, materialize a fake letter to get out of a law suit, when she had offered her apologies to both Frances Sargent Osgood and Samuel Osgood and the revelation that the letter was fake?

There are conflicting dual sides to the Poe, Ellet feud, one by Carol Mattingly and by others, like Thomas Dunn English, compared to Kelly Keener, who is affiliated with the Edgar Allen Poe Society. Likely, as the 2015 anonymous bidder, she bought Ellet's autograph album. Osgood's letters to Ellet and Elizabeth *Ellet's* autograph album were both in the *collection* of Kelly Keener. These items were privately *sold to* the Edgar Allen Poe Review, by Kelly Keener, North Carolina State University. Note that Keener claimed initially that Ellet's autograph book was purchased by an anonymous buyer. Keener refers to Ellet as "one of Poe's vindictive enemies." Not so according to Carol Mattingly nor any other female member of their literary group.

Despite her literary achievements, charitable work and being the first female to write *The Women of the American* Revolution, Ellet was demonized by Poe and Rufus Griswold, but she had the support of women members of their literary group, including Margaret Fuller, Anne Lynch Botta and Anne. S. Stephens, who verified that Poe's wife Virginia showed Ellet incriminating letters from Poe to Osgood, which have been deemed fake. With the permission of Osgood, both Fuller and Lynch visited Mrs. Poe to retrieve the letters that could harm her reputation.

The story, as it's conveyed by the Poe Society and Kelly Keener, who wrote a blog for the Poe Society, is one-sided. Now, more importantly, Keener's response to the letter dated July (7) 8, 1846, is illusive. The letter in the public domain discredits the legitimacy of the letter Ellet was shown by Virginia Poe and likely the letter Maria Clemm showed her at a lady's tea party she had at their house. Keener quoted Ellet, but failed to include the critical reveal, that the letter shown to Ellet by Mrs. Poe, one assumes Keener is referring to Virginia Poe, because Keener has never acknowledged that Maria Clemm also showed Ellet letter(s), which Ellet deemed fake, supported by others researching Maria' Clemm's actions related to the letter ordeal.

Kelly Keener included this portion of the letter: *"Be assured I shall preserve utter silence in future on the subject... only saying... that you have been traduced, wrongfully."* Ellet continues, *"Most fervently do I hope you may soon forget the whole painful affair—that your health & spirits may return,"* responses that clearly correspond with Osgood's letter."* **Elizabeth Fries Ellet**

Kelly Keener left out this portion of the letter: *"Mrs. Osgood has been grossly misrepresented." The Letter shown to Mrs. Ellet by Mrs. Poe must have been a forgery. Ellet retracts her charges about Mrs. Osgood's relations with Poe, and regrets her acquaintance with such people as the Poes."* **Elizabeth Fries Ellet**

In "Edgar A Poe, A Biography, Mournful and Never-Ending Romance," by Pulitzer Prize Winner, author Kenneth Silverman, he verifies Ellet's apology to Osgood and disclosed that the letter read to her by Virginia Poe was a forgery. According to Mr. Silverman, Poe's account of what transpired was that Ellet should be concerned about her own letters, which was "likely a lie." Poe never produced any of Ellet's letters, subsequently Poe apologized for slandering her and retracted his accusation. This was also not included in Keener's response "In Missing Letter Found." As was the case with any disclosure of what transpired that was not in agreement with the Poe point-of-view.

Nevertheless, it wouldn't change the fact, Poe and Osgood carried on visible romantic ties. In that era, it did not favor Osgood's reputation. Yet, while the Poe Society is crediting Virginia as the love of his life, his many romantic dalliances permeated his existence. It's likely that Poe's well-known romanticizing supplanted what must have been unfulfilling romantically under the covers, concerning that aspect of his marriage to a wife who was not well.

In *Missing Letter Found*, Keener depicted Osgood as a "renegade muse," who "captivated men with fantasies that they might recapture their lost inspiration and regain their footing among the literary women." Osgood availed herself as more than a woman puffing the interest of both Poe and Griswold for publication of her work, while still married and likely pregnant. Today she could be referred to as a sidechick, with the coquettish alure that few men could avoid. That was her persona, so let's not make her out to be non-compliant, she was a co-collaborator. What's worse, is Keener's appraisal is sexist, anti-female, demonstrating the separate spheres' mentality of men.

Keener wrote that "Regardless of his, Mr. Osgood's, absences, and despite speculation that the two were living apart, Frances maintained a respectable image and reputation." Fact: they were separated until the summer of 1846 and Samuel Osgood was not faithful to his wife.

To add more dramatic flavor, Keener writes that "It will be noted that, according to Poe, "My poor Virginia was continually tortured (although not deceived) by [Ellet's] anonymous letters, and on her deathbed declared that Mrs. E. had been her murderer." Anonymous Ellet letters now enter the fray without any explanation or proof. Keener conceded this was overly dramatic.

Ellet's concerns for Osgood have been historically interpreted as gossip-mongering by an audience attuned to years of one-sided information, in contrast to the esteemed 19th Century, women writers, publicists, newspaper editors who were part of the literati group who backed Ellet's concern for Osgood. As previously stated, it was Poe who was no longer invited to attend Botta's soirees, as a clearer picture of the concerns for Osgood were revealed. The letters in question, now deemed fake, have now become part of a Poe reveal attempting to perpetuate a storyline. Considering Ellet's defense of women, her own Christian beliefs, it's unlikely Ellet did anything other than puff Poe's interest.

Kenneth Silverman's portrayal of Ellet is intriguing, and it's no wonder the Poe Society and Keener left out what appears to be a more truthful, less biased account of her. He commended her for her independence in not being identified with the feminist movement, referring to them as females seeking notoriety, which as we now know she likely intentionally concealed her feminist connects from public view, while writing exclusively about women for women. Silverman recognized her multi-volume *The Women of the American Revolution* and for being the "first white female to make the hazardous northwest trip to Lake Minnetonka in Minnesota," and he referred to her as "formidable, knowledgeable," and a "zealous Christian with "strict religious observances, unblemished moral training and conservative ideas." But, as you can imagine this translated to "righteous, meddlesome, thieving and vindictive," according to Silverman. The "many" fits in with Griswold and Poe, in particular and others whose misogynistic behavior is recognized in her book *Summer Rambles in the West*.

What's an amazing switch is Poe's estimations of Ellet from laudatory appraisals to outright hatred, which is an intriguing and not a well analyzed change of mind. Evidently during the earlier time frame of their relationship Poe praised Ellet's writing, referring to her as "one of the most accomplished of our countrywomen" and giving her work placement in the expiring Journal during the magazines last two months, assigning Osgood to a less prominent exposure according to Kenneth Silverman. At the time, Silverman, wrote, "it's unclear what the status of the relations were, but that Poe's reluctance where Osgood was concerned may have resulted in Osgood's jealousy." Osgood remarking that Mrs. Ellet, "asked an introduction to him and followed him everywhere." Concerning Ellet's letters to Poe, Silverman's wavelength mirrors mine, Poe likely materialized them, my words.

What is not widely known is that Poe's relationships with other women vexed Osgood. In Poe's interactions with Whitman and Estelle Anna Sarah Lewis, Osgood felt "they exhibited a presumption of intimacy, exemplified a taint of ownership with her patron, Poe." Osgood was fixated on stamping out the claim Lewis wrote "Annabel Lee" a poem published two days after Poe's death. Osgood resented women, who she perceived as competing with her for Poe's attentions. Poe's life was filled with women desirous of publication in the *Broadway Journal*. Poe wrote a poem to Marie Louise Shew who had helped him take care of his wife and lent him money. He had a bevy of women caring for him and his wife when they were ill. In a poem Osgood wrote to Poe before reconciling with her husband, her intent was to retain his affection without harming their reputations. It appears Osgood was covetous of his attention, while rebuffing other female writers who sought publication in the Broadway Journal or complimentary critiques in Godey's Lady's Book. But these revelations are missing from the Poe Societies' telling.

Poe's romantic dalliances spanned throughout his life, the only lasting relationship, likely out of necessity, was his marriage to his cousin, Virginia Clemm. Poe moved into the Clem home after he was expelled or left West Pointe, depending on which version you read and he was kicked out of the Alan family's home in Richmond, eventually marrying his 13-year-old cousin Virginia Clem and moving to Fordham with Virginia and her mother Maria Clemm Poe to avoid the ensuing gossip of the letters.

After Virginia's death in 1847, in the summer of 1848, Poe was courting Mrs. Nancy Locke Richmond (whom he called "Annie") and composing poetic valentines to Sarah Helen Whitman and Marie Louise Shew. Poe was twice engaged to Sarah Elmira Royster Shelton an adolescent sweetheart, the first time in 1826 and the second time in 1849, shortly before his death and before Osgood's death in 1850.

Poe extended a marriage proposal to writer Sarah Helen Whitman in 1848. She turned him down after discovery of his reputation and drinking.

Nancy Richmond, the wife of a paper manufacturer in Massachusetts met Poe in July 1848 when he lectured at Lowell. Although their relationship remained platonic, Richmond and Poe experienced a mutual attraction. Poe called Richmond by the name of "Annie" and wrote his "For Annie" poem for her.

In Joan Dayan's, *Poe's Women: A Feminist Poe?* she notes that "few critics have analyzed Poe and feminism, because his ideas of femininity or womanliness they seem to accept, not question, the brute sexualization and reification of women in the nineteenth century."

Dayan wrote that, "rather than defend Poe's private life or justify his compulsively repeated terms of endearment, I want to reflect on (Virginia) Woolf's portrait of a man hollowed out, exhausted, and unbelieving. For this rather unlovable lover, he wrote "love poems" that would involve him in significant poetic exchanges with Frances Sargent Osgood and Sarah Helen Whitman."

In 1917 Virginia Woolf published an essay in the Times Literary Supplement on Caroline Ticknor's book Poe's Helen (1916). Woolf was more carried away by "the figure of Mrs. Whitman" than by what she described as the "tedious letters" of the "discreditable romantic Poe." "She takes his letters and his love as examples of how Poe, whether he intended it or not, pays the price of stock idealization," as identifying with excessive, imagined perfection.

To view Poe as a womanizer who was drawn to womanliness, e.g., beauty, gentleness, indicating all the behaviors demonstrated by

Osgood, it becomes clear femininity represented what Poe saw in Osgood, not feminism, two disparate interpretations, the latter representing the social, political, economic independence of women entailing distinctions that must be drawn in any consideration of Poe's relationships with women.

Frances Sargent Osgood, a poet, popular in her time was separated from her husband, when she was first introduced to Poe in 1845. Poe gave his first public reading of "The Raven" on *July 19, 1845*. In 1846 Poe contributed many critiques of writers in New York's Literary Society. After the Poe, Osgood scandal, the women of their literary group shunned him. He was no longer invited to weekly soirees resulting in his Literati series in Godey's Lady's book with complimentary critiques he wrote about some of the women in the literati group, with the exclusion of Ellet in his final series in Godey's Lady's Book.

Concerning Victorian parlance, sociocultural cant, currying favor like puffery, acting overly solicitous, which we are not immune to in the 21st century, it was a common tool of Poe's. Poe the journalist frequented the practice of affectionate, doting tributes for the monetary returns many ladies were willing to part with. In a letter to Jane Ermina Locke on May 19, 1848, he "dallied coyly, held out intriguing possibilities, yet evaded positive commitment." To Sarah Anna Lewis he wrote fervidly: "My dear, dear Mrs. Lewis - My dear sister Anna (for so you have permitted me to call you)... I feel for you the purest and profoundest affection - ah let me say love."

Joan Dayan wrote that "Poe could romance and recycle his beloveds in letters, poems, and tales," while still relaying his criticisms of women writers. As an example, as editor of Graham's Magazine, he introduced the American public to the poetry of Elizabeth Barrett Browning (an English Romantic poet, in keeping with his style of writing) who contributed to its pages. His review of Barrett's poem in The Broadway Journal in 1845 demonstrates his awareness of how women writers are treated when "the race of critics," as he puts it, "are masculine - men." Nevertheless, Poe doesn't spare Barrett his criticisms, for he respects her as an equal. Poe said, "The greatest evil resulting from the absence of women critics, he explains, is that "the critical man" finds it "an unpleasant task... 'to speak ill of a woman,'" which couldn't be further from the reality of Poe's behavior, as it pertained to women he didn't like, that he felt were not his equals, that didn't share his literary credo, such as Fuller and Ellet. Whatever may have come out of Poe's mouth, there was always a more truthful alternative.

In his literary interactions Poe was not above responding to below-par writing with the promise of financial recompense. He confessed to Mary Gove-Nichols, who was an author, a holistic health practitioner and a woman's rights activist. Poe told her, "A literary critic must be loath to violate his taste, his sense of the fit and the beautiful," which he did for recompense.

And this is the man, with his eccentricities prevalent in every aspect of his life, accusing Ellet of writing provocative letters to him, of prolonging the gossip about Osgood and Poe. After more than a centennial, what appears to be more about keeping Poe's narratives alive for profit, but certainly not for the benefit of truth, the Poe Foundation, Poe Society, Poe Blog perpetuating untruths and there are Poe Public Schools in several states with the Poe name. The Poe Foundation is a history museum that made $339,362.00 in 2020, imprinting their interpretations of that literary era, solely in their domain. Its mission, along with the Poe Society, is to extend a one-sided view of history, benefiting him. As an essentially primary source, it also has the benefit of defaming Ellet, even as I write, as she is still their main target.

The irony is that Poe, the womanizer, resolved he would no longer pursue quid-pro-quo with female writers to the "last of his tragic days." Mrs. Shew-Houghton, who was Mrs. Poe's nurse, who escaped a murder prosecution, described his occupational anguish, "Mr. Poe expressed to me the great mortification it was to him, and I, childlike, I hated the fat, gaudily dressed woman [Mrs. Lewis] whom I often found sitting in Mrs. Clemm's little kitchen, waiting to see the man of genius, who had rushed out to escape her, to the fields and the forests... I remember Mrs. Lewis in Mrs. Clemm's kitchen waiting for him. I found him sitting on his favorite rock muttering his desire to die and get rid of literary bores (a person who insists in talking about themselves)." How ironic, considering it was Poe's job as a publisher and critique.

Via other sources aside from the Poe Society, even in Poe's own literary contributions, we see the real Poe unfiltered, from his own words. We could ascribe dastardly, fickle, mendacious, addict in comparison to his own, often laudatory self-assessments, but like the narrator in "The Black Cat" who "describes himself as a kind and loving child, a great lover of animals, who then began to change as a result of excessive drinking," which bears no affiliation with the Poe Society formed to adulate him, beyond fact and reason.

Poe's women, per separate spheres, were categorized, their opinions of him reflecting the undeniable double standard of behavior. Mrs. Osgood said this of Poe, "the chivalric, graceful, and almost tender reverence with which he invariably approached all women" (W, I, 295). To Susan A. Weiss he said: "I cannot point an arrow against any woman." In his review of Elizabeth Barrett Browning's, *The Drama of Exile*, Poe quoted Sir James Puckle, British inventor of the Puck Gun or defense gun in the 18th Century, to the effect that "a well-bred man... will never give himself the liberty to speak ill of women," adding "The inherent chivalry of the critical man renders it not only an unpleasant task to him 'to speak ill of a woman,5 (and a woman and her book are identical,) but an almost impossible task not to laud her ad nauseam."(W, XII, 1).

It's as if there are two Poe's, because his self-professed amiability toward all women, is of course a well-documented fallacy, a gross overstatement. Poe disdained feminist, literary women, and women whom he disagreed with, like those actively involved in Transcendentalism, Women's Rights, fawning female writers who sought out his praise and publication, if they didn't fit his ideal woman, his literary style. Any attempts to draw attention to his compromising, illicit behavior concerning Mrs. Osgood, was in that era, in that selective environment, intolerable. Rufus Wilmot Griswold, who it appears was also a serial womanizer, extended future marriage to two other women while married to his current wife, at the time. However, Elizabeth Fries Ellet in particular and others like Thomas Dunn English would not be silenced by these misogynistic indiscretions.

Poe gave high rank to few, just to his favorite female writers including Catharine Maria Sedgwick and Frances Sargent Osgood in the New York Literati. Comparatively Sedgwick, not Osgood is bested today, while women writers he initially praised, then maligned because of their beliefs, moral certitude or calling attention to his romantic dalliances, like Fuller, Ellet, and Ann S. Stephens, and other female members of the Bluestocking, Literati, are studied and read today. His critiques and personal objections to the literary worth of writers, of course extended to both male and female. Being a critique was both a hindrance and a magnet, when applied to Poe's female or male contemporaries. He was referred to as the "Tomahawk Man," relating to his harsh critiques in his time, as compared to how people see him today, mostly as a writer of short stories and mysteries. Poe believed his standards alone applied to every writer.

Adding context to Poe's preferences, for example Frances Sargent Osgood, *In Her Fair Fame: The Reputation of Frances Sargent Osgood, Woman Poet Author*, Mary G. De Jong wrote about exactly what we see for ourselves today, that Poe practically canonized a female poet whose poems are not read today. Poe's personal reputation declined because of his association to Osgood and the fact that he saw worth or promise in what became the uncanonized poems of someone who caused him so much trouble, speaks volumes about his obsessional, self-destructiveness. One critic referred to Osgood as writing sentimental, usually bad poems, as a "not sweet, innocent girl." This is an interpretation along with others, we don't read about, because it's contrary to a manufactured retelling of Poe's literary and personal history.

Poe accused Longfellow of plagiarism, surmising that same charge applied to Mrs. Ellet, though he said, "he had not felt sufficient interest in her works to investigate whether that was true," an example of his penchant for the disdain of two well-known writers of his era, while he was accused of exhibiting "carping littleness" in criticizing the works of others…"

In *Plagiarism in Poe…* by Fernando Galvin, his conclusions were there was some "slight imitations, no plagiarisms" in Longfellow's work and "that criticisms had been dealt with a spirit of illiberality, acrimony, and utter want of fairness, that the only effect of this attempt to hold him up to censure, as an object to be hunted down, like a noble stag, by the whole set of literary bloodhounds, (Mr. Poe as a hound's man), has only served to show how much easier is assertion than proof…" Longfellow never responded to Poe's accusations, but "Poe fabricated a response from Longfellow in order to keep the polemic alive."

In consideration of Poe's response to Longfellow, how Ellet fared after Poe's outlandish, but atypical 19th century, separate spheres public retaliation against her concerns, ultimately resulting in public condemnation of Ellet because Poe accused her of writing similar letters to him. Knowing what we know now about Poe's penchant to manufacture alternate realities, both in his work and in his life, this appears very unlikely.

So, what's really changed in over 150 years, concerning female rights, male, female relationships, entanglements, not much! Women's rights are under assault today, even though they're making more money than men, women still take on the housekeeper, child caretaker role, and there are still issues that remove women's freedoms. Why are some people, so-called conservatives, Republicans, delineating women's rights in the 21st Century, while men's rights remain uncontested, with the exception of Josh Hawley, a United States senator, who wrote a book about men's rights being undermined.

The connections one could make in concluding Elizabeth Fries Ellet's 19th century persona, isn't all that different from those of us who straddle the social mores of what it means to be a woman today. We want the same freedoms men have, with our career choices, the ability to make our own decisions when it applies to our bodies, marriage choices concerning new no-fault divorces. Ellet, like women today are forced into either or positions, just to be accepted. Ellet was a traditionalist, adhering to some of the aspects of True Womanhood because it involved her literary acceptance, and her religious beliefs, but certainly in a less public manner, she was in support of the growing feminist movement. Her actions supported her concern for Osgood's reputation, her involvement in Griswold's divorce case, by siding with his wives, and Ellet's elimination of Catharine Maria Sedgwick, from her book *Queens of American Society,* because she was a single woman, dating men, in an era in which it was not acceptable. Ellet did not publicly become more involved in the women's rights movement itself, only peripherally by being a conduit. Interestingly, Sedgwick faced a similar identity chasm as Ellet, by being single, a status not accepted in 19th century society at her age. Ellet was highly educated, proficient in languages, and was not submissive and wouldn't allow men to subjugate her independence, and her self-assuredness, neither would Sedgwick.

An essay by Mary Kelley, "A Woman Alone" begins with the following claim: "The life of Catharine Maria Sedgwick was betwixt and between." In Kelly's study of nineteenth century "literary domestics," Kelley claimed that "Sedgwick's own position as a single woman left her feeling "unnatural," alone, and in a state of domestic "crisis" (Private Woman, Public Stage 239)."

Maglina Lubovich wrote in *"Married or Single": Catharine Marie Sedgwick on Old Maids, Wives and Marriage,* that "Sedgwick sought to legitimate the status of unmarried woman; it is clear that her true sentiments lay in the home. In saying that the greatest fulfillment for woman was to be found as a wife and mother, she was automatically ascribing an inferior status to the unmarried woman, despite her protests." She too struggled, as many women must have in that era of separate spheres that are still present today.

Chapter 5

*Saucy Escort Cards, Gossip, Mail: A
Writers' Lifeline 1837-1901 Victorian
Era*

They were often called "acquaintance" or "flirtation" cards, which
provided 19th-century singles the ability to alter the rigid rules
of social interaction and elude the formalities of the Victorian Era.
Acquaintance cards came from men and were given to women at a
meeting or attending an event or social gathering as an introduction,
as compared to the usual protocol of an introduction from a friend or
relative.

In the 1850s there were mail collection boxes in hundreds of lo-
cations attached to lamp posts or buildings and the pickup was four
times daily. Sealing wax and wafer seals were used to seal letters before self-gummed envelopes in 1867 were invented. A wafer seal box
sat next to a writer's ink pot with home-made wafers transparent in
appearance.

In 1845 New York's post office was in a Middle Dutch Church,
a 200-year-old structure. It wasn't until 1857 that President Lincoln
gave Congress the authority to build a new post office. Before the post-
al act of 1845, letters were carried by independent letter mail compa-
nies to avoid federal mail charges. There were also hundreds of mail
collection boxes available in 1858. In New York mail boxes were in

street-side shops and businesses. Courtships and romantic dalliances also played a prominent role increasing mail deliveries, such as Elizabeth Barrett and Robert Browning and affairs of the letters like Edgar Allen Poe and Frances Sargent Osgood, though both were married, Osgood was separated at the time.

It's important to point out that Ellet's semi-support of the Cult of True Womanhood, did not deter her from supporting women's rights, nor recognizing their creative and scholarly endeavors, which Ellet has been cited for her dual positions, which exemplified the importance she felt for maintaining some of the ideals of what True Womanhood entailed, while simultaneously standing for women's independence. But as one can discern, letter writing became a point of contention in the 19th Century era when letters could come back and haunt you.

In literary circles, there was a fear of the "bluestocking" ladies, who were educated, literary women. This is exactly the kind of woman, Griswold, Poe and others criticized. But Frances Sargent Osgood's flirtatious wiles were not, according to Poe and Griswold. Only those accused of intellectual pursuits, such as that of the "Bluestocking" ladies, Fuller Ellet, Stephens, and others were given warning by non-other than the publisher of Godey's Lady's Book, Sarah Josepha Hale, not to allow their intellectualism to interfere with God.

If one is to believe Griswold's version of Osgood in her memoir *Reminiscences of Poe* after her death, there are explanations in Burton A. Pollin's "Frances Sargent Osgood and 'Saroni's Musical Times' that show that Griswold's version doesn't correlate with Saroni's original version. Griswold reprinted 'Saroni's Musical Times' without Saroni's permission. As executor for both Poe and Osgood, he likely made changes that didn't reflect accurate dates nor their statements. For instance, Griswold's rendition of Osgood's memoir *Reminiscences of Poe* was addressed to Griswold, not Poe, with a different heading than its first version. Osgood entrusted Griswold with writing her memories of Poe, at a time when she was close to death. Griswold had no reason to change his own sentiments related to Osgood's "envious calumniators," Ellet and Maria Clemm, Virgina Clemm Poe's mother. When it came to who sought who in the Osgood Poe relationship, Osgood wrote it was Poe who sought her affections, not her. She also defended Poe's conduct related to all women, certainly a one-sided assessment of Poe. Griswold, who was enamored with Osgood, was hardly an unbiased participant and executor of Poe and Osgood's collections, resulting in Poe as the enemy and Osgood the femme fatale Griswold had sought, with altered dates and likely context and changes to Griswold's version of Osgood's *Reminiscences of Poe* that Osgood wrote for Poe.

In Pursuit of Possibility, Elizabeth Ellet and the Women of the American Revolution, by Gretchen Ferris Schoel, who used the Poe Society as a source, she relayed that Griswold "puffed" mediocre writers just to retain an alliance with them. Unsurprisingly, "most authors assailed those who threatened their name," which included, "gossip, satire and embarrassing truths, just to hold their opponents at bay." Which is a verification of the undo judgements of female authors who did not hold sway with Griswold or Poe.

What is revealed is that the treatment of female writers like Ellet, Stephens, Fuller and others, was rarely if ever assessed with impartiality, but disdain for their feminist views or their lack of attractiveness. Schoel, is clear, that all condemnations of Ellet emanate from the very men who blamed and demeaned her for citing and countermanding their chauvinist behavior. None of the women in the Literati group, with the exception of Osgood spoke against Ellet, nor women's rights activists.

Chapter 6

Frog-Pondia and Poe's Love Hate Propensity

Poe spent almost 10 years opposed to the intellectual, aesthetic, and cultural principles of New England Transcendentalists, of which Margaret Fuller was a member, though she praised his work and gave him positive critiques, in turn Poe to a much lesser degree. This ambivalence and contempt that Poe demonstrated was doled out for anyone who disagreed with him, a consistent source of animosity, stemming from his dislike of his contemporaries in New England. He considered them enemies, and his attacks resulted in the 10-year 1840-1849 "Frogpondian" War. Poe wrote to Helen Whitman, once fiancée, poet and ironically a Transcendentalist, that "they knew him least and were his enemies," in his *criticisms of Bostonians, New England Transcendentalists.*

Poe called Longfellow a "plagiarist," Emerson a "mystic for mysticism's sake," and he called Carlyle's prose worthless "twaddle." Another favorite target was Margaret Fuller, a Bluestocking, transcendentalist, feminist, abolitionist, and first editor of *The Dial*, the Transcendental, Feminist quarterly. One could say, withstanding Poe's romantic alliances, his disdain for the literary men, including Griswold and women in his aura, were blameworthy and abhorrent in his reality. It's noteworthy that it was Margaret Fuller who accompanied Ann

Lynch Botta to retrieve letters from Frances Sargent Osgood, letters Poe's wife and her mother had shown to Ellet. The concern was for Osgood's reputation, but Poe labeled all the women involved, not just Ellet, as "heartless, unnatural, venomous..."

The irony of Poe's dual adoration and demonization of women, in his work and in life, either dead or silent in his writing, while surrounded by loquacious, intelligent females, including Mrs. Elizabeth Fries Ellet, Catharine Sedgwick, Lydia Sigourney, Elizabeth Oakes Smith, Margaret Fuller, Anne S. Stephens, Ann Lynch Botta, Lydia Maria Child and others, is confounding, a love, hate propensity, perhaps the result of his mother's and foster mother's deaths.

Yet, "Poe wrote about women writers; he wrote to women writers; women writers contributed heavily to both the journals that he edited and those to which he contributed; he attended the literary salons of women writers; he became romantically involved with women writers."

The articulate, out-spoken women, ones who Poe found the least worthy of his regard, were also unattractive, in his eyes, overzealous in terms of their opposition to the separate spheres thinking of 19 Century men. The result was to interpret the allure of women writers based on what has been said about him that "physical appeal at the expense of their words," which is not exactly the same as the male movie producer, the men which were in charge in the movie industry and still are to a great extent, but it's close enough. Considering Poe's and Osgood's exchange of poems in the Broadway Journal, what has been referred to as a "literary courtship" is in keeping with her well-known coquetry, but if there was more going on than an interchange of words, his special interest in promoting her, this was still an infatuation that even Poe's wife is said to have supported, according to the Poe Society. Virginia Poe looked upon Osgood as a backup in the event she died. If the Poe's, Osgood's letters were innocuous, why then did Osgood release Poe's letters and choose not to defend them, and where are all those letters? Did Osgood and Poe have an illicit affair, considering from 1830 to 1890, there was a growing debate over adultery and marriage as it pertains to fidelity. It obviously was a matter of concern for women then, when considering the dictates of male dominant expectations, considering the values held to the separate sphere's mentality, the chaste female ideal. The concept that women could not have paramours, but men could while married, was not beyond the preferences of the 19th Century male, while women were expected to be obedient, soft spoken. But for many women in the feminist wave of literary women, in particular, they had outgrown that requisite male provinciality.

A women's physical appearances were paramount to Poe, even as an editor, critic, at the cost of suppressing the words of those women who did not appeal to him. Poe's criticism of most women writers was mostly ignored by other editors and critics. In Daniel Hoffman's words, "Poe's own standards were not only high but a little odd: he couldn't keep himself from overpraising poetesses who wrote elegies to dead lovers." Likely a reference to the poetess and member of the New York Literati, Frances Sargent Osgood.

In Poe's Women: A Feminist Poe? Joan Dayan describes Virginia Woolf's 1917 assessment of Poe's letters to Mrs. Whitman, as "tedious letters of the discreditable romantic," referring to Poe's letters, whether intended or not as "stock idealization." Woolf wrote, "He might have been addressing a fashion plate in a lady's newspaper - a fashion plate which walked the cemetery by moonlight, for the atmosphere is one of withered roses and moonshine." Dayan writes the Woolf that Poe describes is "a skeptic caught in a haze of lies, opium, and alcohol, a man who "had no emotion left about anything, "a man who was, to use one of Poe's favorite phrases, "used up."

Dylan Thomas wrote, "If women exist at all in Poe's letters, tale, or poems, they appear to be excuses for this continued fascination with himself. It is not surprising, then, that many complaints about Poe's poetry, like those of T. S. Eliot or Yvor Winters, focus on his "excess of sentiment, his preoccupation with his own mood."

Chapter 7

Poe's Indulgences, Libel Suit and the
End of New York Literati

Once a prominent member of New York's Literary Society, Edgar Allen Poe achieved national recognition after the New York Mirror published his poem "The Raven" in 1845, with a mere $9 recompense for writing it at the time. Poe became editor of the *Broadway Journal*, a weekly, published from 1845 to 1846 which contained Poe's writings and critiques of other writers.

Poe's literary background also includes The Southern Literary Messenger, Burton's Gentleman's Magazine, American Monthly Magazine, American Museum of Science, Literature, and the Arts, and published in many others like the Dollar Newspapers, Godey's Lady's Book, and the Broadway Journal, over which he had editorial control for a short time. Poe wasn't only a writer and poet; he was a critic. He often expressed a dislike for the work of fellow authors, resulting in the nickname, "The Tomahawk Man."

In April 1845 Poe published Elizabeth Fries Ellet's "Law and Waltzing," translated from French and six poems. Ellet studied German, French and Italian and often wrote letters in a language other than English. One small piece of a letter, a part from the main letter asking if Poe would publish an article about the Dean of a South Carolina College, who was being fired, was in German asking Poe to call for her at her residence, in what was purported to be flirtatious. That portion of the letter was not Ellet's handwriting and more recently was considered by Poe online (Letter Date Dec 16, 1845), to be a mistake.

After the Poe and Osgood's affair of the letters, in which Poe faulted Ellet, even though this was about her concern for Osgood, which is evident in multiple examples of Ellet coming to the aid of women in trouble included in this book. Poe retaliated and eliminated Ellet from his final series on the Literati of New York writers in *Godey's Lady's Book*.

Poe's critique of Margaret Fuller's *Woman in the Nineteenth Century* (1845) as a work he considered "unmitigated radicalism" and as "nervous, forcible, thoughtful, suggestive, brilliant, and to a certain extent scholar-like," though it does not sufficiently consider "the intention of the Deity as regards sexual differences," inferring that God never intended an equal status for women.

How this sheds light on Poe's relationships with women, not unusual in that era, adds further relevance to 19th century male spheres of patriarchy. Poe was certainly not alone, Nathaniel Hawthorne ridiculed Fuller after her death, referring to her as a "humbug" lacking the charm of womanhood."

In Thomas Dunn English's *Reminiscences of Poe* [Part 3] *Independent* (New York)1896, English wrote that Poe's wife had learned of Poe's relation with Osgood, which was causing concern, jealousy among the women at Botta's soirees. English, while in attendance one evening, described Mrs. Ellet as "decorous and ladylike," while Mrs. Osgood was seated on a footstool in front of Poe with her face turned up in adoration. Mrs. Maria Clemm, Poe's wife's mother, contacted English and asked if he would intercede and uncouple what appeared to be a liaison beyond literary matters. It was suggested that Ellet should say something to Poe about it, which did not go over well. Poe was angered and others suggested Poe should return Osgood's letters. Poe accused Ellet of mischaracterizing his relationship with Osgood and accused Ellet of writing questionable letters to him. Dunn defended Ellet, saying "there were no such compromising letters, and that she was a gentlewoman of undoubtedly unblemished character with manners, esteem and respect from all her associates."

"In Punish with Impunity: Poe, Thomas Dunn English and the Cask of Amontillado," right from the beginning, 1841-1842, Poe and English's relationship was marked by personal differences. English has visited Poe and published complimentary reviews, but Poe's drinking, and his behavior were unacceptable, being that English was a tea-drinker and even published in a temperance journal, and wrote a novel *The Doom of the Drinker* (1847) in which English described Poe as uttering "some brilliant jest," while "under the excitement of wine," even as being "a man of a higher order than ordinary genius, yet, one who appropriates the ideas of others and is the very incarnation of treachery and falsehood."

The Thomas Dunn English, Poe tit-for-tat did not end there, eventually in 1846, Poe and English's relationship ended when Ellet's brother challenged Poe to a duel. Evidently Poe not only asked for English to lend him a pistol, but he wanted English to be his second, if needed. Charges English made about a loan and forgery were evidently false charges, resulting in Poe successfully suing the *New York Mirror*. English and Poe never met again after interchanges English deemed unacceptable.

In Buford Jones and Kent Ljunguist's Poe, Mrs. Osgood and "Annabel Lee," they believed there was no relationship more complicated, rife with both fact and fiction than Poe's relationship with Osgood, who is said to have "taken the initiative in the flirtation."

Poe's relations with the New York literati declined after the affair of the letters became the subject of gossip in literary circles. Poe appeared less frequently at literary gatherings. Miss Lynch, who, according to Mrs. Elizabeth Oakes Smith, was strict in drawing the moral as well as the intellectual line, wrote after Poe's death, in an apparent allusion to Mrs. Ellet, that she had seen little of Poe in his last years, a consequence of a wide difference of opinion between us in reference to his treatment of ladies at the literary gatherings. Poe found few female defenders in the affair of the letters, and the general opinion seems to have been that he had impeached the integrity of an innocent woman.

Poe was removed from guest lists which resulted in a decline of his popularity and reputation. Poe wrote to Thomas H. Chivers he had "been driven to the very gates of death and a despair more dreadful than death, and I had not even one friend, out of my family, with whom to advise." The incident did much to darken Poe's life and reputation during his few remaining years, and his literary enemies kept the matter fresh in the mind of the public.

Despite his popularity downtrend, Poe's Literary sketches were mostly well received. His criticisms of the New York Literati in Godey's Lady's Book were met with both enthusiasm and trepidation. There were some good reviews and the realization that Poe, "hatchet man," had been an out-cast whose published opinions might well be marked by ill-feelings, and this was certainly true in Ellet's regard, who was excluded from his review.

In Braddy, Haldeen and Yannella, D. J. Reviews of *Poe's Major Crisis: His Libel Suit and New York's Literary World*, by S. P. Moss, they reveal the rejection and the culmination of Poe's ten years of critical warfare as a magazine critic and editor in New York. Poe's downfall was proliferated by hundreds of court records, newspaper articles, letters, diary entries, detailing Poe's literary demise. From 1846 to 1847 Poe sought refuge at Fordham cottage, suffering illness and enduring poverty, the death of his wife in January of 1847 and the ruination of his personal and literary reputation. Poe's own literary battles, and there were many, from 1845 to 1846 and press runs of Poe's private life and his "War of the Literati," resulted in a continuance of court appearances.

Poe knew New York was the only place to realize his goal to create a magazine, but the competition of *Godey's Lady's Book* and *Grahams Magazine* were obstacles. Through his relationship with Duyckinck and his friends, and the Young America Group, Poe was provided a new avenue, but his independence and critiques of others continued to defile his reputation. Regardless, with Duyckinck's help Poe's *Tales* and *The Raven* were published in 1845. Poe was not well known and not popular, so publishing work that wasn't aligned with the mission of the Young America group, intent on putting out national literature, led by Duyckinck's democratic leanings, was the antithesis of Poe, who discredited the influence of nationality on American critics and audiences.

Publisher and biographer, Duyckinck's letters about Ellet give us a sense of who she really was as compared to her male calumniators. Dr. Ellet's letter on Ellet's wishes to leave South Carolina corroborated by Everett Duyckinck's letter attests to William Henry Eller as a devoted husband.

Nevertheless, Poe praised Young America after sullying it, then he accused himself of flippancy,

writing, "could I imagine that, at any moment, you regarded a certain and flippant critique as more than a matter to be laughed at. I would proffer an apology on the spot."

Poe's alliance with Duyckinck's Young America was suspect, as he was referred to as an erratic member and more desirous of starting a 'War of the Literati,' against the Knickerbocker Group.

Poe had become known for his aggressive and unfamiliar attacks on magazine coteries, using criticism as a weapon to create literary alliances.

It's likely that the combination of Laudanum, which contains opium and whiskey contributed to Poe's behavior. In Yewdale's *Edgar Allen Poe, Pathologically*, he wrote that Poe's drinking quelled his sorrow, allowed him to sustain human relations and mitigate those feelings. Poe was not one of the guys, but more of a loner, though it was the intrigues of his many affairs with women that were public fodder for the rest of his life.

In a letter to Mrs. Whitman, Poe wrote likely after the death of his wife, "I have absolutely no pleasure in the stimulants in which I sometimes so madly indulge. It has not been in the pursuit of pleasure that I have periled life and reputation and reason. It has been in the desperate attempt in escaping torturing memories."

Yewdale writes, "Poe was by nature a solitary man and apparently, he visited very little, showing his want of animal spirits and aversion to society. But whisky altered him, for in his letter to an unknown friend he wrote, "The desire for society comes upon me only when I have become excited to drink. Then only I go-that is at this time only I have been in the practice of going among my friends, who seldom, or in fact never, having seen me unless, excited, take it for granted that I am always so."

After the demise of the *Broadway Journal*, Poe's solitary support ended, he then created an avenue that would allow him to be both creator and publisher, with the introduction of *The Literati of "New York City in Godey's Lady's Book,"* and he did this by prompting gossip among the Literati with a combination of the *"The Raven"* and the publication of two of his books. After that the ladies were spellbound by favorable critiques and fellow authors, editors began frequenting the soirees more often. But in 1846, Poe threatened to publish what was intended to be private communications. He did not reveal who these communications were from, which was perceived as deceitful. It cost him his reputation, as he became the object of "spiteful gossip and abuse."

To provide context, according to Carol Mattingly in *Legacy File, Elizabeth Fries Lummis Ellet, 1818-1877,* the affair of the letters between Osgood and Poe began when Poe was editor of the Broadway Journal from 1845 to 1846. At the time Poe and Osgood were regularly attending events and social gatherings together while both were married, Osgood was separated at the time. Were the letters from Osgood that Poe threatened to publish or Ellet's? Did Maria Clemm sell or dispose of the letters in question?

Gaylord Clark, editor of the *Knickerbocker Magazine*, also self-appointed overseer of New York's Literary reputations referred to its author, Poe, "today in the, tomorrow in some milliner's magazine." Clark said, "Poe exceeded all too well in creating the journalistic success he wanted."

James Russel Lowell wrote in a *"In the Question of Poe's Narrators,"* this…"to accept him as a really serious writer, Lowell's flashy indictment of Poe as "two-fifths sheer fudge," agrees essentially with Henry James's magisterial declaration that an "enthusiasm for Poe is the mark of a decidedly primitive stage of reflection."

In *Poe's Major Crisis,* by Moss, Lewis Gaylord Clark wrote, "Poe no doubt, would have agreed that he had practiced a dubious morality in betraying or threatening to betray the confidences for "The Literati," but he would also have argued that his object, for all the impurity of his motives and the "occasional words of personality," part of his subtitle to "The Literati," which "adulterated his purpose was indubitably moral – the purification of American criticism."

Chapter 8

*Griswold's Divorce Case with
Charlotte Meyers Griswold and
Elizabeth Fries Ellet, and Ann S.
Stephens Involvement*

Rufus Griswold

Griswold was many things, editor, critic and executor of Poe and Osgood's estates. He was also a womanizer and likely committed bigamy in a time when men, especially men of influence, could stack the legal deck against you.

Rufus Griswold

Griswold's 19th-century separate spheres behavior wasn't tolerated by Stephens and Ellet, in their defense of Griswold's wife, Charlotte Meyers Griswold. Ann and Ellet wrote letters to two women, Alice Craig and Harriet McCrillis, who both expected a proposal of marriage to Griswold, while he was still married to Charlotte Meyers Griswold. In the recent republishing of Griswold's notes on the divorce from Charlotte, he excoriated Ellet for sending letters to women she didn't even know, without his permission.

Both Anne S. Stephens and Margaret Fuller, female members of the New York's Literary Society, who Poe said Ellet had forced them to retrieve his letters in Osgood's possession, joined Ellet again in defense of Charlotte Meyers Griswold concerning Griswold's divorce case. Rufus Wilmot Griswold believed Fuller went against his notion of femininity, describing her as "an eloquent expression of her discontent at having been created female."

Stephens who got involved in the Griswold divorce case with Ellet, was once an associate editor alongside Edgar Allen Poe at *Graham's Magazine* in 1841. In 1846, Stephens became part of Poe's Literati. What her position alongside Poe invariably entailed, aside from her work, were contradictory appraisals of her writing. For example, Poe said that her style lacks "real power through its verboseness and floridity," adding her "sentences were too long," yet he ascribed her as a "high talent if not genius," than noting her "plumpness, beautiful eyes and blond hair." In 1857 Ellet took over Stephen's place at the *New York Evening Press* (Express (1836-1881) newspaper.

Griswold was married three times: his first wife Caroline Searles, who he had two children with, died young, *his second marriage to Charlotte Meyers Griswold ended in a public and controversial divorce*, and his third wife Harriet McCrillis left him. Rufus Griswold married McCrillis in 1852. McCrillis had Griswold's male child in 1853. McCrillis soon left Griswold, who died in 1857, leaving her nothing.

There are of course different renditions of Griswold's marriages, two sources which eliminate them by Jacob L. Neu in a 1925 publication, *Rufus Wilmot Griswold*, University of Texas Press, which makes no mention of Griswold proposing to two women at the same time, while still married, nor does Wikimedia's version from Joy Bayliss.

Interestingly a book written about Griswold and Charlotte Meyers, is Rufus Wilmot Griswold's own account, originally written June 9, 1856 and published in 2012, *Statement of The Relations of Rufus W. Griswold with Charlotte Myers (called Charlotte Griswold,) Elizabeth F. Ellet, Ann S. Stephens, Samuel J. Waring, Hamilton R. Searles, and Charles D. Lewis, With Particular Reference To Their Late Unsuccessful Attempt,* with the clear intention of vindicating himself in perpetuity, by discrediting Ellet and Stephens who interceded on Charlotte's behalf.

Not surprising that another female from the era of separate spheres, Charlotte Meyers Griswold, is still being accused falsely of accusing Griswold of undue behavior in his relationships with women, including her defenders, particularly Ellet over 150 years later, involving a one-sided retelling of what occurred between the sheets in the Griswold's bedroom. The argument against her was that she was incapable of sexual relations. How do we know that on Griswold's say alone, aside from Charlotte, who has no current voice in the matter to attest to her sexual prowess, therefore her voice is underrepresented, overridden by what is likely an inaccurate representation of what actually occurred.

Because now we also know that Griswold was entangled with poet Alice Cary, another reason why he wanted to end his marriage to Charlotte. Before Cary could entangle Griswold, he married Harriet McCrillis. Ellet was aware of this, and it's likely why she, and Ann S. Stephens, fought on behalf of Charlotte Griswold. Also indicative of the support Charlotte had, Griswold's first wife's brother, a lawyer, Hamilton R. Searles, was active in Charlotte's defense, credit to the Special Collections, Addlestone Library, College of Charleston.

In 1852 Griswold took steps to divorce Charlotte, "due to his disinterest in her and increasing interest in Alice Cary," In Review of

Female Poets, by Ernest S. Leisy, we know Cary moved to New York due to *an interest in Griswold*; however, Cary also knew New York as a literary hub. She also continued her correspondence with Griswold and confessed her attraction to him. She suffered another disappointment when he married another woman late in 1852." That would be Harriet McCrillis.

Joy Bayless, Rufus Wilmot Griswold's literary executor, in a Wikipedia entry, wrote that Charlotte's lawyer drew up a contract "to separate, altogether and forever," which would in effect be divorce. The contract forbade Griswold from remarrying (as he was attempting to do by courting, offering marriage to two other women while married, which is bigamy) and paid him $1000 for expenses for his daughter Caroline staying with the Myers family." This attempt by Charlotte didn't succeed, but it does reflect on the now voiceless, former Mrs. Griswold. His next wife, Harriet McCrillis, also left him. What we know are several reasons why Ellet and Stephens pursued a divorce on Charlotte's behalf, reasons that could involve Griswold being an unfit husband, father and committing a decidedly immoral transgression by extending marital promises to two women while married.

In a fascinating, gossipy newspaper article, credit to the Special Collections, Addlestone Library, College of Charleston, describing the Reverend Rufus Griswold divorce case, the author uses the word **apocryphal** when referring to the documents that Charlotte Meyers Griswold's lawyer would present. A friend of Griswold suggested his lawyers would buy a judgement decision favoring him. Charlotte's lawyer was accused of "oily hands" inferring dishonesty and providing "false bait" to win the case, suggesting rumors were used as bait against Griswold. In what reads like a **who done it**, heavy-handed article without an unbiased perspective, atypical of that era and ours when it comes to these situations.

Could a woman win a divorce case, particularly against a famous writer, in an era where divorce in New York required serious multiple charges as the only avenue to end a marriage? Considering Griswold had proposed to two other women and is said to have been enamored with poet Ann Carey, more than likely all the reasons for wanting to divorce Charlotte.

Another unsurprising reveal about Griswold, he was unrepentant, exhibiting an artifice of innocence to the very end in the republication of his final statement in a book published October 22nd 2022, its contents in the public domain, publisher Legar Street Press. It's a thirty-three-page self-defense of Griswold's case against his second wife, Charlotte Meyers Griswold, with a postscript by Griswold from New York, June 9, 1856.

> *This pamphlet was written, and nearly printed two months ago, and soon after the publication of the above opinion, relieving me from the imputation of any undo means in obtaining a divorce. The publication of the pamphlet at the time would have gratified, no doubt, a morbid public appetite, and led to a much more extensive and interested reading of it, than it will have now. But such appetite I have not desired to gratify. And I have knowledge of other people's private concerns, has passed away. I design it for those sober-minded persons - whether my friends or otherwise - who take a sufficient interest in the truth in what has been brought before the public, to read a statement on the subject with the same interest, now, as when it was the talk of the town." To them I submit it.*
> *June 9, 1856*

These thirty-three pages should be considered with the perspective of Griswold's penchant for lies, contextual vacancies, proposing marriage to two other women, and a romantic interest in the Poet Ann Carey, with a book title that's a give-away: *Statement of the Relations of Rufus W. Griswold With Charlotte Myers (Called Charlotte Griswold,) Elizabeth F. Ellet, Ann S. Stephens, Samuel J. Waring, Hamilton R. Searles, and Charles D. Lewis: With Particular Reference to*

*Their Late Unsuccessful Attempt to Have Set Aside the Decree Grant-
ed in 1852 by the Court of Common Pleas of Philadelphia County, in
the Case of Griswold Vs; Griswold.*

On page twenty-five Griswold wrote: "As I have said, I received,
in due course, on the conclusion of my suit for divorce, a communication from my counsel that the decision of the court had been in my
favor, with his congratulations on the occasion."

With his divorce from Charlotte just finalized December 18, 1852,
Griswold married Harriet McCrillis on December 26. A month later
Ellet accused Griswold of bribing the Pennsylvania Legislature, Ellet
obtaining the knowledge of the circumstances, and caused Griswold
to be arrested for bigamy. Griswold was courting and offering marriage to two women, Harriet McCrillis and Alice Craig while married
to Charlotte, which is not mentioned in Griswold's account, though
he did accuse Ellet of writing letters to two other ladies, she didn't
know, (which would be McCrillis and Craig) related to the divorce of
Charlotte. There were also laws at that time which forbade women to
retain ownership of pre-marital property in a divorce, which Charlotte
possessed and would lose to Griswold, but Griswold did not include
this in his divorce agreement. While men could more easily sue wom-
en for adultery, women had to show their husbands were incestuous,
physically cruel and adulterous.

To retrace the Griswold Charlotte Meyer extremely brief marriage, in 1845 Griswold was approached by the aunts of Charlotte
Meyers to marry her. In August of that year, he said his "indisposition
to marry Charlotte had increased due to reflection on the matter." Griswold professed he did not love her and likely couldn't and Charlotte
responded, saying "love grows as a relationship deepens." Griswold
persisted in his objection, and the Meyers family followed him to New
York on the 20th of August. A marriage service commenced, followed
that night, according to Griswold, with the knowledge that Charlotte
had been "bound in honor and law, not to receive any man's offer of
marriage." Griswold resolved to immediately end the marriage. There

was a common law in the 19th Century called coverture, which allowed a woman's legal identity to be transferred to her husband, which would imply divestiture, but Griswold's divorce documents made clear that Charlotte's propriety would not be subsumed by him. Did Griswold fabricate the law used to overturn his marriage vows, related to Charlotte's vow not to receive any man's offer of marriage? Coverture was a law that married women were incapable of owning property or making a contract.

In Law, Sex, Cruelty and Divorce in Victorian America, 1840 -1900, Robert L. Griswold, not Rufus Wilmot Griswold, yes, exceedingly ironic, wrote that in these legal cases, jurists didn't see sexual satisfaction as essential to marriage. This is important, because Rufus Griswold's contention was that Charlotte was incapable of sexual relations due to some physical infirmity. Maybe that's what he was referring to when he posited Charlotte was "bound in honor and law, not to receive any man's offer of marriage," drawing a veil over the truth to serve his own interests. At the time jurists did not see sexual deprivation as a divorceable offense, nor excessive carnal demands as a divorceable offense. But knowing the law, Griswold's entire defense must have been paid off to ensure, regardless of the laws, that he would win the case.

Griswold, the author, goes on to describe, what's not that dissimilar when compared to our current reversal of women's rights, with no-fault divorce now under consideration, but opposed by conservative lawmakers on the basis it would destroy the family unit. Nineteenth Century jurists were ultimately supportive of two spheres, one to enforce conservative estimations of marriage in what was still completely patriarchal, as it applied to family life and sex roles. However it was also an era of transition, indicated by the women's rights movement, concerning sperate spheres, gender roles, a family transformation that had legal repercussions with women usually bearing the brunt, which Griswold, the author, was intent on sustaining the old social order vs women as new domestic contributors, women able to control their sexuality, fertility, the need for men to soften their patriarchal grip, all assessed together multiplied the eventuality of separation, divorce. We see this female movement toward more freedom even being squelched today. What was 19th century sperate spheres thinking still hovering over women in the 21st Century. A YouGov 2023 poll indicates that 34% of Americans describe their ideal relationship as something other than complete monogamy. Eighteen- to forty-four-year-old women are the largest non-monogamous category and the same goes for men in that age group, 2nd in line, an interesting factoid.

Today, so-called conservative politicians are against no-fault marriage because it impacts the family unit, which is a flash-back to 19th century separate spheres. In consideration that most marriages today end in divorce, for a multitude of reasons, including a lack of commitment, infidelity, lack of intimacy, conflict, and more single families are headed by moms today. This is not the 19th century, and not the Leave it to Beaver 50s era. Marriage through the centuries has evolved from Stone Age pairing, to polygamy, to the Holy Union of the Church, to the separate sphere's marriage, and monogamous households, which was more a Western propensity. And the notion that single motherhood discrimination that existed in the 19th century, but does not today, is totally inaccurate.

The sperate spheres era in which Rufus Griswold sought a divorce, with his rules and his witnesses, jurists and judges who all agreed, and because he was Rufus Wilmot Griswold, he held sway. His witnesses all verified Griswold's account of the divorce; a Mr. Samuel A. Harrison testified he had boarded at the Butler House on Chestnut Street, and he had not observed them acting cordially and others had remarked they slept separately. Mr. Francise II. Janvier testified that his impression was that their separation was a permanent one. Hon J.R. Tyson, L.L.D. testified as lawyer in regard to Griswold wanting Charlotte to retain her property. Another lawyer testified, Hon. J.R. Tyson, L.L.D., his opinion was it was a short time after the marriage to assess whether a divorce should be terminated. The Reverend Herman Hooker, D.D., a witness who testified on behalf of Griswold, also stayed at the Butler House and relayed similar observations, which supported Griswold, that he showed signs of mental affliction, that he and Charlotte didn't share a bedroom, nor dine together.

At a time when traditional female gender roles were changing, strong-minded, determined, independent women like Ellet, Fuller, Stephens and other writers who attended Botta's soirees were met with more resistance by men, not coincidentally, just when women were beginning to demand an equal voice, equal rights. It's also possible that Poe and Griswold, who both shared an infatuation with Frances Sargent Osgood, poet and member of the Literati Group at the time, were likely perturbed by Ellet and her literary friends' concerns over married men conducting dalliances with a married woman. Poe, in particular, was angered after Ellet made his behavior more widely known to female friends in the Literati Group, upon discovering a letter from Poe to Osgood, but their behavior was observed by all, real letter, fake letter or no letter!

Griswold and Poe were very much a part of the same New York literary scene at the time with Ellet and other Bluestocking literary ladies, who were aware of and concerned about an ongoing flirtation referenced in the *Broadway Journal* and at private meetings between Poe and Osgood, including the knowledge of letters between them. Margaret Fuller who was one of the most important feminists of her day, also belonged to the New England intellectual community called the transcendentalists, which included Ralph Waldo Emerson, Henry David Thoreau and Anne C. Lynch Botta, who introduced Poe at her literary soirees. Lynch and Fuller helped retrieve Osgood's letters from Poe, which resulted in an enraged Poe, who exacted his revenge by excluding Ellet from his famed "The Literati of New York City," in *Godey's Lady's Book*.

Griswold was already irritated that Ellet didn't give him more credit for introducing her to officials of the New York Historical Society, where she obtained some of the historical background for her book

The Women of the American Revolution. It certainly didn't help that Ellet and Ann S. Stephens, American novelist, magazine editor and author of Dime Novels acted as witnesses on behalf of his third wife, Harriet McCrillis, during divorce proceedings. By 21st century conventions concerning moral standards, Griswold would be described as a cad and you don't have to brood over that realization, because being a cad is still an attractant for some women today.

Ellet pursued her career without the overt submissiveness of some other females, but with self-assuredness and authority, which evidently angered both Poe and Griswold. She was praised for her translations, poetry, the sheer amount of her publications, and as the first women to delve into the history of American women during the Revolution, she and other women, were in essence, moving into some of the literary roles of men, hence the antipathy toward women, who were not in Griswold's estimation, "capable of the same intellectual prowess."

In Griswold's thirty-three, page statement on his divorce to Charlotte Meyer Griswold, he indicates their conjugal relationship was never consummated, for the first time the inference is that it was not because she couldn't perform sexual relations, which has been a continuous defense, now, according to him, this arranged marriage was not his choice, after-the-fact, so Griswold immediately went about terminating the marriage. Now, it comes down to, which version to believe?

Griswold was editor to the most well-known authors of the time and was under the tutelage of Horace Greeley during his first foray into editing. A historian in his own right, Griswold published *The Republican Court*, a study of social life in Washington's administration. He was a journalist, critic, anthologist, and editor who co-edited *Graham's Magazine* with Edgar Allen Poe. He is said to have been quarrelsome and emotional in his dealings with others.

Poe and Griswold's tempestuous relationship, from its beginnings to Poe's death and beyond, resulting in Griswold still slandering Poe after his death, likely the result of Poe's severe critiques of Griswold's work as well as their mutual attraction to Osgood. Griswold was Poe's literary executor, a relationship that didn't end well, which is true of most of Poe's and Griswold's relationships, particularly with women. Like Poe, Griswold held a 19th century view of women as belonging to a different sphere, which excluded them from participating in historically male roles, like writing, editing, reporting. Certainly, conjugal relations in the 19th century, despite being described as an era of flirtatiousness, was the domain of men, as was their authority over their wives.

Griswold was executor of both Poe and Osgood's literary estates. *In Frances Sargent Osgood and "Saroni's Musical Times": Documents Linking Poe, Osgood and Griswold,* "Osgood said, this collection of my poems is from previous publications and manuscripts by a literary friend, presumably Griswold." While the letter of contract with Griswold and the publisher Carey and Hart of Philadelphia, was extant at the time.

What we know is that Poe was likely behind the publication of Osgood's poetry collection. In Poe's review of her 1845 Poems in March of that year in Godey's Lady's book, he wrote of Osgood, "with the carelessness which seems a portion of such character she has done herself gross injustice by failing to take proper care of the children of her delicate fancy, by suffering them to run wild, unheeded and forgotten by herself, so that many of them are perhaps irrecoverably lost. *In Frances Sargent Osgood and "Saroni's Musical Times: Documents Linking Poe, Osgood, and Griswold* by Burton R. Pollin, we learn that Poe repeated this charge in the "Literati" paper on Osgood in September 1846: "Many a goodly reputation has been reared upon a far more unstable basis than her unclaimed, uncollected "fugitive pieces." It would appear, Poe's attentions, romantic or not, whether it was Virginia Poe, Francis Sargent Osgood or any of Poe's many dalliances, professed love interests were never everlasting!

Also, In Frances Sargent Osgood's "Saroni's Musical Times": Documents Linking Poe, Osgood, and Griswold Author(s): Burton R.

Pollin wrote that Griswold had fabricated what is now a non-extant letter, altering its date with a request from Osgood to "write the life of Poe." Griswold responding that he would do as she wished to "put down at once my envious calumniators…Mrs. Ellet [and Mrs. Clemm] …I wish the simple truth to be known, - that he sought me, not I him." It goes on, claiming it was Poe who sought her out, it wasn't consensual… writing "imploring me to love him, many a letter which I did not reply to until his wife added her entreaties to his…"

The only aspect of this that's true is that Mrs. Maria Clemm, Virginia's mother, showed her concerns, however self-serving it was, to Ellet about the Poe, Osgood relationship. After the affair of the letters and Lynch Botta's soirees dropped in attendance, Osgood still remained covetous of Poe's admiration, attentiveness, despite the fact their relationship had ended and they never saw each other, which does correlate with her intense adulation and defense of him. Poe moved on, courting other women after Virginia Poe's death in 1847, Poe died in 1849, and Osgood died in 1850. Whether the response, Poe sought her, not the other way around from Osgood, who was not well, or it was Griswold's interpretation, we may never know.

Chapter 9

The Cult of Domesticity, Cult of True Womanhood, Separate Spheres, Feminism

The period of 1820 to 1860 saw a rise in America of an ideology of feminine behavior, an ideal of what a woman should be that came to be known as the "Cult of True Womanhood" or "Cult of Domesticity," which prescribed female roles of domesticity to women of upper and middle classes. Ellet's books couldn't be clearer that her focus was on women's lives apart from separate spheres, which were essentially imposed on women, by men, including some of her more popular and well-known books...

The Women of the American Revolution I, II, III
Domestic History of the American Woman
Pioneer Women of the West
Rambles About the Country
Women Artists in all Ages and Countries
Queens of American Society
New Cyclopedia of Domestic Economy, and Practical Housekeeper
The Eminent and Heroic Women of America
Summer Rambles in the West
Teresa Contarini

In a re-review of *Women Artists in all Ages and Countries,* by Sandra L. Langer, she apprises Ellet's work as feminist, thus requiring a feminist interpretation. Ellet, unlike some of her male contemporaries, gave women their rightful place in history rather than ignore or devalue their contributions. Ellet revealed, through meticulous research, the forgotten history of America's founding women, giving women an active role in both the nurture and defense of what would become the new country, where everyone had the potential to play a role that was not prescribed, regardless of their gender, which remains unfulfilled today, going back, over two hundred years later.

Ellet was committing a revolutionary act by writing about and reviewing women artists and writing the history of *The Women in the Revolutionary War*, but according to her detractors, Rufus Wilmot Griswold and William Gilmore Simms, who called themselves historians, they failed to acknowledge that women in America had been writing history since the 18th century. Nevertheless, writing about history and women artists world-wide was considered the sole domain of men. And when that male dominated genre was challenged, history writers she sought advice from Griswold and Simms, who both gave her sources on her book, *The Woman of the American Revolution*, but were angered by what they deemed a lack of attribution. What resulted were rumors of plagiarism. No such accusations came from others, like James Fenimore Cooper, an American novelist, famous for his *Leather Stocking Tales* and Jared Sparks, an American historian, Educator and Unitarian minister, who Ellet also contacted for guidance and sources for her three-volume work, *The Women of the American Revolution* (1848-1850), the first history of women's participation in the American Revolution, which also included corresponding with Susan J. Donaldson, Eliza Susan Quincy, Delia Tudor (Stewart) Parnell, and Lucy Knox Thatcher; prominent politicians and writers including Robert J. Breckinridge, John C. Calhoun, Henry Clay, George Washington Parke Custis, and Washington Irving; and noted historians of the day such as Henry Onderdonk Jr., William Hickling Prescott, and

George Washington Greene, grandson of Catherine Littlefield Greene and Revolutionary war hero Nathaniel Greene, according to the Library of Congress.

What Ellet also accomplished as a writer was to present a "readable text," a women's only text about women, which Poe denounced, referring to Ellet's writing as "rifacimento," a recast, adaption of something else that was written. What's fascinating about Ellet is that while she was revealing women and female artists not constrained by the "cult of true womanhood," she personally (to a certain extent) conformed to it, for example as it pertained to certain standards, for instance by not including Catherine Sedgewick in her book, *Women Artists in all Ages and Countries,* because she was a single woman dating men. Essentially, Ellet's stance was that "females chose to be artists rather than objects." Ellet's intent was likely to give attention to and cause for other young women not to deny their talents in a field of male artisans, not unlike Ellet and other women in New York experiencing a literary coming-out into a male dominated literary scene. If Ellet's position was that a single woman dating men was unacceptable behavior, it's incongruous to posit she would enact a romantic dalliance or such an intentional interest in Poe, beyond puffing his interest in publishing opportunities, but not as the Poe Museum, the Poe Society and the Poe Foundation continue to propound intentional romantic interest.

In "Thomas Hardy and the History of Friendship Between the Sexes," by William Deresiewicz, he details the 19th Century behavior of male, female relationships, friendships, that he referred to as "contemporary phenomenon." The introduction of women into literary circles, like the New York Literati group of writers, was the beginning of friendships among "educated and or well-born people." Friendships were non-existent before the 19th century, related to male, female friendships.

Friendship between the sexes would not adhere to historic European traditions, mainly because women were viewed as subordinate, also because male, female relationships revolved around sex. Friends were relatives, spouses, benefactors. British author and women's rights advocate, Mary Wollstonecraft, 1759-1797, warned against male/female friendships, that women should learn skills to support herself and her children without marriage, and become more educated. Concerning dating in the 19th century, there were open houses where men and women met. Ads were placed in newspapers, and there were strict rules about visiting someone, which had a time limit. There were also Saucy Escort Cards as way to meet someone, other than an introduction by a family member or a friend. But dating, as it's referred to today, inferred a proposal, a long courtship, particularly among the wealthier and more educated class.

Considering what was historically radical in altering the roles women had been tied to, which included only the perspectives of men, "19th century feminist intellectual revisionism" was about the removal of prototypes associated with what females could and should do. This was a male dominated stance Ellet and the Bluestocking literary ladies were surrounded by, related to New York literary men, whose notion of marital fidelity was exclusionary, could and wives couldn't. And when it came to a woman's position in the literary world of that era, a perfect example of separate spheres, is that Ellet couldn't write history, but Rufus Wilmot Griswold could.

At the heart of legend": Feminist Revisionist Mythology in Twentieth Century Poetry, an Honors Thesis by Madison Rozells, he clearly identifies women's rejection of inequitable gender roles preserved by men. These are roles that are still foisted on women today, particularly by Republican elected officials, men and women, who don't support the Equal Rights Amendment. Rozells's thesis is focused on 19th century female revisionist poets, and of how women then were ineffectual, as "emotional, (irrational), weak, nurturing and submissive," while men were "rational, strong, protective and decisive." It's entirely straightforward in recognizing these stereotypes even today. To further elucidate this male propensity to impose these limitations in current terms Rozells includes this from, Ahmed, Sara. "Feminist Killjoys."

The Promise of Happiness, Duke University Press, who wrote, "these gender roles have been used very unsuccessfully to justify inequities, which still occurs today."

Though Ellet was certainly demonstrating feminist thoughts and actions, she did not take a publicly known activist stance in the feminist movement herself as discussed in other chapters, other than to be a conduit, a helper (that we know of) in demonstrating her interests, which lied solely in helping women in need. Susan Phinney Conrad's *Perish the Thought: Intellectual Women in Romantic America*, 1830-1860, wrote about the personalities, problems and cultural contributions of Ellet's contemporaries, Margaret Fuller, Lydia Maria Child and Elizabeth Cady Stanton, and that Ellet in comparison may be seen as a committed feminist still holding on to both the restrictions of True Womanhood and the emancipation of women in the Women's Rights Movement.

From the standpoint of revealing the accomplishments of women artists conveyed by a woman to a female audience, not to other authors or audience experts, it reveals Ellet's understanding of her audience and what they had been deprived of. Ellet was writing for every woman, in ways men couldn't. This was obviously not appreciated by her most vehement critiques, Edgar Allen Poe and Rufus Griswold nor was her penchant to do what detectives and reporters do, information gathering, which was often referred to by Poe, Griswold and others as meddling. Considering Ellet took over at the New York Evening Press newspaper as an editor, taking Anne S. Stephens place, and her involvement in the protection of women fleeing their abusive husbands, and ensuring their rights, it's not surprising, considering much of her communication skills were used to represent and defend women.

In "Between Domesticity and Revolution: Inherent Contradictions in The Early Women's Rights Movement," by Laura Neylan, she validates Ellet's book, "A Domestic History of Women in the American Revolution," for describing the virtuosities of women inside the home and "audaciously" describes their virtuosities outside of separate spheres. Neylan wrote just the fact that Ellet's focus was women in a male dominant era was historically significant.

During the Revolutionary war, women's actions had to be affirmed by their husbands. In one passage a woman could bake, but she could also fulfill roles men traditionally assumed. As obvious as it seems today, in both the Revolutionary era and post-Revolutionary era, Ellet depicts women functioning both inside and outside of their stereotypical gender spheres. They followed behind their soldier-husbands in wagons, women spied on the British and performed deeds in support of the Militia, Minutemen and Continental armies. Ellet also associated women with domesticity and femininity. Regardless of which typically male roles women assumed during that period, domesticity was still her domain by Ellet's definition. Neylan classified Ellet as a proponent of the cult of domesticity.

My contention is that Ellet was certainly straddling spheres in her own life. Not in Ellet's era, but today, depending on your personal and political views, you could aspire to be whatever you choose depending on your own beliefs and independence: feminine, domestic, bearer of life or not, soldier, politician, truck driver. But with existing political drawbacks today from conservative, religious and political entities, the 19th Century is being reinserted back into women's lives.

Deborah L. Rotman PhD, wrote in *Separate Spheres,* a separate female and male sphere existed, one of domestic duties such as raising children, care for the household and all that conveyed and the public economic sphere, which men dominated. Clearly then, women had scant ability to effect social change, particularly ones associated with their own rights, rights they did not have, for instance rights related to owning property, legal rights to their children, voting, and working outside the home and having the control over money they made. It wasn't until 1848 and the historic Married Women's Property Act in New York, that women were able to control the money they earned in that state, the first state to do so.

Emily Dickinson

Emily Dickinson

Dickinson was definitely aware of separate spheres and wrote about in *A Man may make a Remark*, 952.

A Man may make a Remark -
In itself - a quiet thing
That may furnish the Fuse unto a Spark
In dormant nature - lain -

Let us divide - with skill -
Let us discourse - with care -
Powder exists in Charcoal -
Before it exists in Fire -

Though Emily didn't experience the acclaim and popularity of her work, she is one of the most popular and oft read poets of her era. She was a gardener, an observer and lover of birds. With Emily's unique dashes, dots, capitalization and unexpected vocabulary, her poetry is eclectic, and are compared to "crossword puzzles, enigmatic and unforgettable."

Emily Dickinson, 1830-1886, a contemporary of Ellet, knew she lived in a woman-wary culture, one of two-spheres, when the phrase, "true womanhood" or the "cult of true womanhood or domesticity" was mentioned in magazines as often as God was in religious periodicals. Like the poems Emily Dickinson wrote, some reveal Dickinson's feminist consciousness, that the "cult of domesticity" made oppressive demands upon women, and she revealed an unwillingness to submit to them. Dickinson wrote Susan Gilbert, her best friend and sister-in-law, that her choice of spinsterhood was from a fear of "yielding up" to wifehood.

Dickinson wrote:

"My Husband"?
women say?
Stroking the Melody?
Is this? the way?"

Dickinson lived for 30 years next to her best loved friend and her brother, witnessing their turbulent unhappy marriage.

Barbara Welter's *Cult of True Womanhood,* 1820-1860 defines antebellum (1815-1861) American women as being held hostage to "piety, purity, submissiveness and domesticity." The "Cult of Domesticity," prescribed female roles of domesticity to women of upper and middle classes. It's clear that Ellet recognized and wrote about all the different roles women played, but the role she created for herself was not one of a housewife or a mother.

This separation of women and men, two spheres thinking, existed among male writers like Poe and Griswold, both maintained an unfavorable opinion of literary women and their writings, with the exception of those they were attracted to, in particular Frances Sargent Osgood, who personified coquetry and though she was married and had children, whether she fit the "cult of true womanhood," label is questionable, since her behavior belied that categorization on the basis of her romantic entanglement with Poe. Griswold, who like Poe, were both inured with Osgood, and couldn't see beyond their own male fixations and refusal to give credit to the literary genius in all women. Poe and Griswold's accrued "feelings mistaken for creative intelligence," in female writers. Both were totally in-sync with dominant male spheres, that female writing and publishing, which was moving in on what had been strictly male dominated, was viewed as an intolerable obtrusion, but not when it came to Osgood.

Poe's fictional women, Floyd Sovall wrote in *The Women of Poe's Poems and Tales,* included grotesque women, which encompassed the message of Hop-frog, which has been suggested as a story of literary revenge against Elizabeth F. Ellet and her circle, in contrast to *A Valentine*, in which Poe wrote about the luminous eyes of Frances Sargent Osgood, which provides a compelling juxtaposition. Granted every man and woman is entitled to their own preferences, but Poe portrayed women darkly and dead and as victims in his poems and stories. And in real life, the filter he used in projecting disdain for women was misogynistic, a separate spheres mentality. Edgar Allan Poe's general loathing, love, hate posture with women, defined his writing and his relationships.

Gaslight Foster, George Goodrich Foster, was a New York Journalist, most active during the 1845-1856 period of New York's burgeoning metropolis with all its beggars and prostitutes, its common people and the Literati, including those in attendance at Anne Lynch Botta's New York Literary soirees, where she hosted literary greats from Longfellow, Louisa May Alcott, Thoreau, Lydia Marie Child, including Margaret Fuller, Edgar Allen Poe, Elizabeth Fries Ellet, Frances Sargent Osgood, Elizabeth Oakes Smith and others.

Foster's boyhood friend was Rufus Griswold, an attendee at New York's Literary Soirees. From 1847 to 1848, Foster gained entry to the New York Literati and his poems appeared in American Monthly Magazine. Foster is also mentioned for his efforts in establishing and contributing to early American humorous publications. But Foster's reporting on New York's literary soirees, particularly Ann Lynch's Valentine party, increased his public audience, with a focus on Margaret Fuller for her connection to Transcendentalism and her advocacy of women's rights and Frances Osgood better known today for her involvement with Poe than for her poetry.

In Foster's assessment of Elizabeth Oakes Smith, a frequent guest at Lynch's soirees, he found that her articles on labor and the condition of women in society, speaking as a man of his times, deemed that a "women's destiny is to be beautiful and musical and not enter into the "rubbish-strewn arena of literature and art."

Instead, True Womanhood was the expectation of every man in the era of 19th Century. Women should personify these 4 categories of behavior, or "cardinal virtues," to include piety, purity, submissiveness and domesticity, which is how women were judged by all of society, including her husband and neighbors, which alluded to a woman's respective titles, mother, daughter, sister, wife-woman with religion at the core of a woman's virtues.

Sarah Josepha Hale

Publisher of Lady's Godey's Book, Hale eschewed the feminist movement. She upheld separate spheres, believing in less education and more religion. Her large readership was exemplified by the content of the books versus new feminist magazines, which had a smaller audience.

Sarah Joseph Hale

Women, particularly women in publishing, writing, the literary arts were given notice that their literary and intellectual pursuits would remove them from God. The publisher of Godey's Lady's Book, Sarah Josepha Hale, chastised those who she believed had thrown away the "One True Book." Hale referred to Margaret Fuller as evidence, "intellectualism risked wandering from the salvation of Christ." Margaret

Fuller was a Unitarian and did not give up her belief in Jesus Christ as her savior. Every possible source refutes Hale's denouncements of the Literary Ladies who didn't exactly conform to her religious views. What's also mentioned in another chapter is that when Ellet's husband was dying, she cared for him, prayed with him, they had a shared belief in faith and God, the comfort of their Christian friends, which made Dr Ellet's passing easier for him.

Nina Baym writes in *Onward Christian Women*, that Sarah Josepha Hale, the Lady's Godey's Book publisher was considered a "backward force, a woman impeding the development of egalitarian feminism by espousing the ideology of separate spheres."

Lady's Godey's Book

Illustrations included steel engravings, woodcuts, and copper engravings of landscapes, flower arrangements typical of that period, family images, advertising of household products, women's and men's clothing and stories and poems written by authors, including the New York Literati.

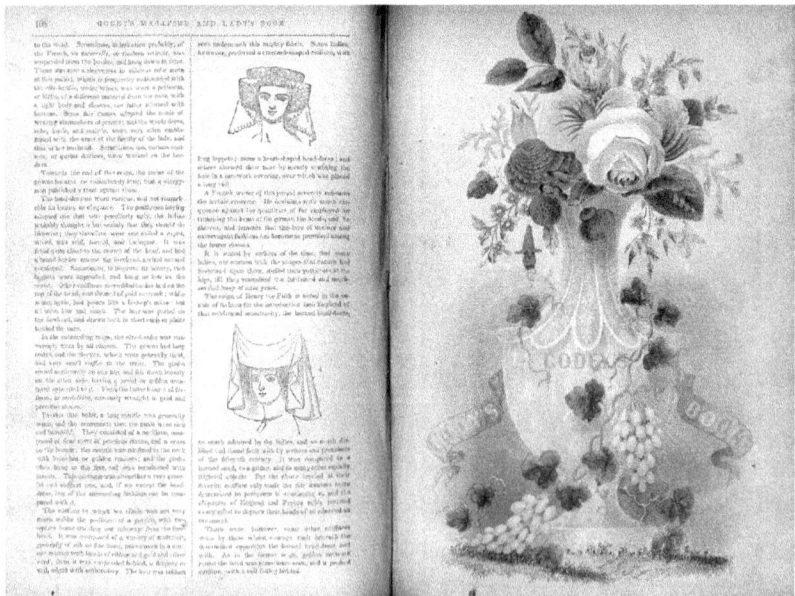

Page from Lady's Godey's Book

In Sarah Josepha Hale's book, *Women's Record*, published in 1853, and in other publications, Hale sets out to promote the "feminine as demure, complaisant, while the book is given over to men, shockingly." Hale wrote that men have "shown in their laws and customs, more respect for women than any other nation." Consider the equal rights amendment did not pass until 1919 and women couldn't own a home, had no rights to their children nor could handle their own money, to name just a few restrictions men imposed on what women could and couldn't do.

Hale also argued the case for female superiority and that women are "God's appointed agent of morality, in terms of sentiments, humanity and virtues, which depend on the manner in which her mission is treated by man." In other words, a high moral ground is one that men have not shown much interest in through the ages. Hale was essentially enabling separate spheres. "In Onward Christian Women: Sarah J. Hale's History of the World," by Nina Baym, she cites Sarah Josepha Hale's book *Woman's Record*, first published in 1853 and revised in 1855, that Hale's resounding message is infused with Christianity to the detrimental exclusion of the freedoms denied women. Hale believed women's rights and freedoms can only be attained thru their religious beliefs.

Ellet's *The Women of the American Revolution,* which literally revolutionizes women's unknown roles in our nation's fight for independence was published in 1848 and has four stars on Good Reads while Hale's book, *Woman's Record* has none. What's so important about Ellet's historical rendition, and I will repeat this, there is no mention of George Washington nor any man, not even her own relative John Maxwell, who served under George Washington. This was a groundbreaking act to exclude men in our founding battle and a first by a woman.

It's 2024, and the Equal Rights Amendment has still not been enshrined in the Constitution, which requires a two-thirds vote in Congress. If as Hale said, that "women are God's appointed agent of morality," why are men and even some women, still holding woman's equal rights back? "On April 27, 2023, Senate Republicans blocked a measure to allow the Equal Rights Amendment to be added to the Constitution on a 51 to 47 vote to invoke cloture on a motion to proceed, falling short of 60 votes needed." The equal protection clause in the 14th amendment means that states must treat all their citizens equally.

Christian Nationalism as it pertains to an ongoing refutation of our rights, whether it be gender roles in the family, same-sex marriage, transgender rights, is contrary to the Constitution, "Congress shall make no law respecting an establishment of religion." In the 19th Century, the moral codes depended on which faction of society, with a consistent reference to religion, "faith, charity, respect" depended on, and who was defining these behaviors has historically been men. At one time "piety, courage and industry," was the moral code, but ultimately moral codes have been constantly redefined. In the 21st century "humanistic values that are "secular, democratic and pluralistic," as behavioral norms do not coincide with Christian nationalistic views.

George Washington Burnap, a Unitarian Clergyman, who lectured on Spheres and the Duties of women in the 19th Century, believed that "a woman feels weak and timid, so she needs a protector, and that she is in measure dependent and asks for firmness, and is willing to repay it all by the surrender of the full treasure of her affection."

Horace Greeley, Founder and Editor of the New York Tribune wrote in his autobiography, *Recollections of a Busy Life* (New York, 1868) that as "noble and great as Margaret Fuller was, a good husband and two or three bouncing babies would have emancipated her from a deal of cant," (the specialized jargon of a particular group, used to mislead others not in their group) and the nonsense, one supposes, of doing what was perceived by men of women doing a man's job.

Margaret Fuller was the first female correspondent in the U.S., the first book reviewer in a U.S. Paper, a woman who fought for "the fullest recognition of social and political equality," for women. Fuller and Emerson edited *The Dial*, the first Transcendental magazine in 1840. Fuller's *Woman in the Nineteenth Century* is considered the first major feminist work published.

Horace Greeley, recognized and praised her aims with the condition, that the "enfranchised woman would free herself from the obedience to etiquette and the need of a masculine arm crossing the street." Greely was of the opinion that until emancipation, that he "could not see the woman's rights theory' is ever to be anything more than a logically defensible abstraction."

In *Margaret Fuller, Body and Soul,* by Cynthia J. Davis, we get another confirmation of 19th century separate spheres thinking by men, as exampled here. Fuller's appearance was "unwomanly" according to one male critic. Davis includes this snippet, In Charles F. Briggs *Women in the Nineteenth Century* in the *Broadway Journal*, Briggs uses the example of Fuller's consideration that Mrs. Siddons, the famed British actress was an "instance of what a woman may affect in public. But Mrs. Siddons came before the public only as a woman, representing always a woman, either as a wife, a mother, or a betrothed wife." Fuller was not a wife or mother at the time. It's clear, that women's expected appearance and lifestyle was the cause of much consternation by 19th century men if a woman did not play the role she was intended to follow, just like Poe's reference to Fuller, that "humanity consists of three types of people, men, woman and Margaret Fuller."

On May 1, 1850, "In printing a full report of the first women's convention, held in Ohio, the New York, Tribune, on May 1, 1850, declared that a sincere Republican could give no adequate reason for refusing the suffrage to women if they should, as a body, demand it, because it was "a natural right, however unwise or unnatural the demand." This view was slightly amended by Dr. Horace Bushnell, a Congregational Minister.

In (reviewed work(s): Women's Suffrage; The Reform against Nature by Horace Bushnell: The Subjection of Women by John Stuart Mill, we learn that Dr. Bushnell 1802-1876), American Congressional Minister and theologian, believed the status of women is one of "wrongful alignment," as it pertains to education and occupation, but where it concerns their participation in governing of "any sort," being resolute in his defiance of what woman could and couldn't do. He goes on to exclude them from being pastors, bishops, attorney's or judges, administrative work of any kind, holding political office, because, "she is not created to mingle in any kind of strife or to batter the servitudes of fortune."

Fast-forward to the 20th Century

In the 1960's, historian Barbara Welter, who termed the 19th century stereotype for women as the "Cult of True Womanhood," referring to "mystique," as its synonym and their "cardinal" virtues as "piety, purity and submissiveness, as a woman's proper sphere."

In Linda K. Kerber's, *Separate Spheres, Female Worlds, Woman's Place: The Rhetoric of Women's History Author(s), 1988,* she clarifies that separate spheres was a metaphor used instead of the "Cult of True Womanhood."

In *Inventing a Feminist Discourse: Rhetoric and Resistance in Margaret Fuller's Woman in the Nineteenth Century*, by Annette Kolodny, 1994, she wrote that "to read Fuller today is to be impressed anew with the sheer revolutionary daring of her attempt both to question existing gender hierarchies and to disrupt accepted sexual practices."

Context, Margaret Fuller and Anne Lynch Botta didn't have to be coaxed or forced by Ellet to visit Osgood and retrieve letters that had the potential to hurt her reputation. Both were disdainful of Poe, both were feminists. Elizabeth Oakes Smith noted that Botta refused to allow Poe to return to her Literary Soirees due to her own moral, ethical stance.

Temperance, Abolitionism, Feminism Aligned in the 19th Century

In Carol Mattingly's Water Drops from Women Writers: A Temperance Reader, Mattingly elucidates on women's positions on temperance and men's unfair laws, and how its impact resulted in "wives' antipathy toward their spouses." Mattingly links "temperance and women's rights in what has been a failure by male historians to link its relevance and how women's reform fiction correlates with the impact of the temperance and the women's rights movements."

What is reform fiction and when did it begin? In the middle of the 19th century, reform fiction, human-interest stories, were exemplified by New York's literati female writers like Fuller, Stephens, and Ellet, all had been newspaper writers and or editors. They and others enlivened newspapers with more than just "daily compilations from political parties to revolving into more of a public forum, which resulted in personal interviews, foreign correspondents, opinions, national health, science coverage and endless opportunities for all voices to be heard," of course depending on a magazine or a news papers' political leanings and or focus on religious issues. The train, telegraph and the improved paper making machine and printing press, and a more educated populace resulted in increased readership and the creation of the penny press.

From Reviewed Work(s): "Water Drops from Women Writers: A Temperance Reader" by Carol Mattingly, she puts it right on the line, that women approached the problems they faced via writing by "attacking vice mostly associated with liquor, men's unfair laws and women's guilt by association with their intemperate spouses." She cites the conflation of alcoholic consumption by men with women's rights and how women authors turned to drink or opium themselves to cope with their marital problems.

Mattingly revealed that Temperance leaders employed what was a popular cause to appeal to lecturers, newspapers, magazine writers, novelists, whose articulations represented the oppression of women in everyday language in order to identify how women were subdued. She wrote, "critically speaking in terms of feminine equality, it was the first-time women had a collective voice." In admiration, Mattingly referred to Harriet Beecher Stowe and Louisa May Alcott, and their contributions as foremothers of today's feminists, which has been ignored by historians.

Inventing a Feminist Discourse: Rhetoric and Resistance in Margaret Fuller's Woman in the Nineteenth Century, by Annette Kolodny, she writes that Fuller found female ani-slavery speakers were better able to reach their audiences than their male piers. While the women spoke in terms of "home relations," compared to the men, who spoke in more "intellectual and combative terms."

Beginnings of a feminist philosophy that formulated Fuller's positions occurred while teaching at Green Street School, Providence Rhode Island, along with her original essay, "The Great Lawsuit: Man versus Men. Woman versus Women," which was in the July 1843 issue of *The Dial* and ultimately was expanded in her book, *Woman in the Nineteenth Century.*

In Fergenson, Laraine R. "Margaret Fuller in the Classroom: The Providence Period." *Studies in the American Renaissance*, 1987," we learn about those early attempts by Fuller for a more progressive education, particularly one that embraced female students in the 1830s, is that Fuller was its sole proponent. She introduced female teachers, as role models, for students and included subject matter with the intent of targeting their interests, revolutionary in its approach versus what was referred to as "mind training via "rote recitation," at the hand of a man holding the "rod and ruler." It was instead an "education by discussion and doing." So, "together with her row of pupils, adolescent girls…" Fuller was intent on creating a "collegial setting of teacher and students, rather than the older hierarchy that set an instructor apart from his pupils."

In Margaret Fuller's "Women in the Nineteenth Century" she wrote it was up to women to take responsibility for other women, advising women to take matters into their own hands, so suspect were men's positions on morals in laws. Mattingly wrote of the travails of women in that era involved in the temperance movement, and the similarity between the issues that the women's rights movement also addressed, both movements contributing more to improve the lives of women.

Not unlike what Sarah Josepha Hale, Godey's Lady's Book publisher said, Margaret Fuller wrote in *Women in the Nineteenth Century* "that women needed to take responsibility for the education of other women, the bulk of these stories advise women into their own hands, so suspect are men's morals and laws."

The 19th Century temperance campaign was the largest movement of women, outnumbering that of suffrage organizations, so it was incumbent on women suffragettes, suffragists to participate in support of the Prohibition Amendment, despite its failure and the contention by some that it was a failure of moral governance.

In *Boundless United States History, Lumen Learning*, addressing Abolitionist News, beginning with *The Emancipator of 1820,* its chief representative in William Lloyd Garrison's Liberator, relayed a focus on slavery, and the struggle for freedom. These abolitionist papers were excluded from mail circulation. Forbidden in the South, in New York, Boston, and other cities in the United States, their editors were assaulted, offices attacked and destroyed. Today, they're excluded or misinterpreted by so-called conservative media. It's not surprising that over the years, there are now fewer black magazines, and the study of Black History is not allowed in certain states. All indicators throughout this book exemplify a return to 19th Century patriarchal, racist, anti-female positions.

In "Teaching about Slavery, the Abolitionist Movement, and Women's Suffrage." Nancy Hoffman references studying the period from 1830 to 1870 linking white women's activism on behalf of blacks, the founding of the Philadelphia Anti-slavery Society and a black rebellion. Nat Turner's Revolt, described as "the deadliest slave revolt against whites in our history, in 1830, before the cessation of the Civil War 1865. What is not widely known, or her support has been mischaracterized, Susan B. Anthony was collecting anti-slavery petitions when she was 17 and became an agent for the American Anti-Slavery Society at age 36.

Post Civil War, suffrage and freedmen were looked upon as a separable, not inseparable, with insurmountable hurdles, for all intents and purposes, a race and sex conundrum. Frederick Douglass said black men would take care of black women and refereed to 1867 as "the Negro's hour." Stanton's reaction was feeling duped since Douglass had supported the Women's Rights Convention at Seneca Falls in 1848.

From my own view of history, I can't concur with Stanton's premise, that whites were native born and blacks were not. Neither were native born. Stone Age hunters, ancestors of Native American Indians have been here 13,000 years ago or longer, according to many sources, including the Smithsonian. The upshot of all the efforts of Suffragettes, and Abolitionists to equalize rights across color and sex is that ultimately the word "male" was inserted in the 14th Amendment. In an author interview on National Public Radio for a three-part series, "For Stanton All Women Were Not Created Equal," Historian Lori Ginsburg commented in 2011, that Stanton prioritized white women. Ginsburg is the author of *Elizabeth Cady Stanton: An American Life.*

In 1967, Aileen Kraditor published "Means and Ends in American Abolitionism," which required historians to reexamine the 19th century battle between black male rights and women's rights, as to suffragettes compromising their own principles. Kraditor was disapproving of suffragette racial positions, but in the greater scheme, her response was that the right to "stand in court, to act in a public sphere, to own property, determine the fate of one's children, those basic rights should be inalienable," no matter your color or sex.

Frederick Douglass wrote in "We Are Men,' that "Antebellum access to American rights and citizenship were qualified by sex and race, thus limited by assumptions who could handle the responsibilities of republican citizenship." It took the fifteenth, nineteenth, twenty-fourth and the twenty-sixth amendments to give everyone an unfettered right to vote. But prohibitions still exist in different forms, gerrymandering, voter intimidation, accessibility, reduced polling place hours, long list…

Competing interests, dependent on your views, and male dominance is likely why men got the vote first. Douglass addressed black women's issues less, exemplifying he wasn't dissimilar to white men, who viewed black or white women as victims, requiring protection, which we've heard countless times from the white male members of New York Literati. Yet, there was the belief, mostly among women, that any communal changes could aid both black women and men. In our current political climate according to Pew Research, "eight in ten black adults say it's as important for women to have the same rights as men, though they support gender equality, they are split on transgender and nonbinary issues," according to research from February, 2023.

The founding of the Anti-Slavery Society consisted of sixty-four male abolitionists from ten of the free states, convening in Philadelphia's Adelphi Building December, 1833. They organized to secure the abolition of slavery in the United States as soon as possible and without any compensation to slaveholders.

Four Philadelphia women, Lydia Mott's cousin, Lucretia Mott, Lydia White, Esther Moore, and Sidney Ann Lewis attended as observers, as they were not recognized as delegates. However, Lucretia Mott spoke and suggested several amendments to the society's declaration of sentiments which the members of the convention accepted. One of the male delegates said later, that he had never before heard a woman speak at a public meeting. Days later a group of integrated women got together in a school room to form an Anti-Slavery Society based on the principles of existing national societies.

Delegates from the Anti-Slavery Society in Pennsylvania attended the World's Convention presenting to the Committee of the British & Foreign Anti-slavery Society, but it turned out that they would not be seated at the convention, which was the very first item on the agenda. Ultimately, the women were allowed to be seated in the gallery. The result of being banished from participating in the proceedings was a critical and long-lasting friendship between Lucretia Mott, abolitionist and Elizabeth Cady Stanton, feminist and women's rights advocate. After the Convention was over, both agreed to work on women's rights and freedom for slaves. Not an interpretation that is the most popular among those who persist in the notion that there was no interconnection between the anti-slavery and pro-women's rights advocates. There's still an ongoing perception, and opinion by many that the temperance, abolitionist and feminist movements were not supporting one another, which appears to be more an issue of competitiveness revolved into a time worn fallacy.

In Nelson, Marjory, "Women Suffrage and Race." *Off Our Back, sh*e wrote that Black middle class, educated women started to organize social and civic clubs to help them respond to the changes in their lives and in the community. In 1896, these clubs consolidated as the National Association of Colored Women, with headquarters in Washington, DC and Mary Church Terrell as first president. Terrell had gone to NAWSA's conventions for years and thought of herself as an "Ambassador" to the white woman's suffrage association. The NACW endorsed woman suffrage.

Stanton and Anthony's reaction to the 15th amendment was betrayal by those who had supported women's rights, including Frederick Douglass, who attended Seneca Falls in 1848, putting his name on the Declaration of Sentiments in support of women's rights. That's when Stanton and Anthony formed the NWSA, which did not exclude African American/black women from membership. Yet many more black suffragettes joined and participated in the AWSA.

What is not widely known is that whites were impressed with Native American women pertaining to suffrage, but the media depicted them as savages, which belied the stature of Native American females in their communities, which included "independence and matrilineal authority."

The reference to Native women as "squaws" ended with white suffragettes' familiarity with Native women. Another not well-known fact, both Elizabeth Cady Stanton and Lucretia Mott, visited Indian communities, both had visited Iroquois land decades earlier. Completely left out of a discussion in the struggle for female rights, Native women, whose "matriarchal political power" impressed white suffragettes.

As to equal rights, the Library of Congress describes it this way, amid concerns that the Interpretation Act 1850 could use *masculine words in legislation "deemed and taken to include females."* To replace the word "man" with "person" in the Representation of the People Act of 1867 which was debated, but later defeated, with 196 voted against and 73 votes for the amendment." The word "male" was ultimately inserted in the 15th amendment.

It wasn't until 1923, that Alice Paul created the ERA, the Equal Rights Amendment, which included a second part, "every place subject to its jurisdiction," which went beyond women and men to include "Indian reservations, U.S. territories, like Hawaii and Alaska, and the overseas colonies, Puerto Rico, Guam, and the Philippines."

It's indisputable, that from the 19th century when, Fuller, Ellet, Stephen and New York Literati ladies, and Abolitionists like Lydia Maria Child, Harriet Beecher Stowe and Lucretia Mott, wrote about issues of women's equality, and defended women's rights not just through their writing, but their actions, it still remains and ongoing struggle in the 21st Century.

Chapter 10

The Young Americans, Transcendentalists, Realism vs. Romanticism

Historical Realism, Dime Novels, Women Write History

Poe moved around the country, from Virginia to New York to find work and escape the debt he incurred to fulfill his ultimate goal and create his own first-class magazine. As it turned out his hopscotching from Boston, Virginia, South Carolina, to New York, Virginia, Pennsylvania, and back again to New York, Rhode Island and Maryland, is where his long and tortured, creative life ended in an unmarked grave in Baltimore, until 26 years later, when he was moved to a place of honor in West Baltimore in 1849. But that was by no means the end of Poe's legacy. One hundred and twenty-six years later in 1923, the Poe Society was founded and the resurrection of Poe's reputation had begun.

Poe began writing short stories in 1832 after moving in with his Aunt Maria Clemm in Baltimore, Virginia Clemm's mother, and Poe's soon-to-be wife. He was an editor for four different magazines in eleven years before he became editor of the Broadway Journal in 1845 to 1846. Poe's initial attempts at being a critic for magazines in Richmond and Philadelphia showed his disdain for someone's else's views and control, a characteristic that never abated, except when it came to the possibilities in New York, the only place with a literary establishment conducive to new enterprises in publishing. In New York Poe could have total control. But Poe needed financial backing and New York was where the money flowed.

Evert A. Duyckinck

Publisher and biographer Duyckinck played a critical part in the careers of 19th century writers and the advancement of literature in that era. He wrote about William Henry Ellet in what is now a biographical document of Henry's interest in selling their house in South Carolina so his wife could pursue her writing career in New York.

Evert A. Duyckinck

With the help of Evert A. Duycinick, the founder of "The Young

Americans," a group of writers at odds with Poe in 1844, Poe sought financial support and guidance from Duycinick in order to compete with Godey's Lady's Book and Graham's Magazine.

One hindrance was that Duycinick believed in a National Literature with a Democratic focus. Duycinick helped found the Tetractys Club along with Cornelius Matthews and the Young Americans, who supported the common man, democracy and reform, with the goal of creating an American literature, rather than one that was a European conglomeration.

The irony, this was not at all the direction Poe was going, this was about Jacksonian democratic principles reaching out to the masses. Walt Whitman supported the politics of the *Democratic Review*, one of the group's publications, and wrote for it as well. Poe did not support a national literature, yet his allegiance to Young America held.

Even after the Raven was published, and Poe's popularity sky-rocketed, the public's appetite for short stories was nil, resulting in scant interest nor profitability, compared to long novels. In the publication of *Poes Tales*, which did not include any new material, readers were more interested in other authors. The irony is that Poe's short stories are more popular and adaptable to all types of media now, which were not available in the 19th century.

Poe supported the group, because it ultimately aided his own self-serving goals, because Poe was the antithesis of "The Young Americans." The group, consisting of authors like Melville, Whitman and Hawthorne, who supported social reforms, which were without question of a Democratic persuasion.

In a letter to one of the "The Young Americans" Cornelius Matthews, a writer and critique, Poe wrote that he accused himself of flippancy, "Could I imagine that, at any moment, you regarded a certain and flippant critique as more than a matter to be laughed at, I would proffer an apology on the spot…"

But that didn't deter Poe from a cut-throat review of Matthews' poem *Wakondah*, Poe wrote, "We should proceed - but how?

to applaud - but what? Surely no declamation, this maudlin senti-ment, this metaphor twaddling verbiage, this halting and doggerel rhythm, unintelligible rant and cant," slang, inferring a derogatory, disrespectful viewpoint of someone or something. Poe had already articulated his objections to National literature, which is beloved today, saying it "perverts the taste of the American public by puff-ing such trash."

Ultimately, Poe's relationships with Duycinick, William Cullen Bryant, Cornelius Matthews and other members of "The Young Amer-icans" were critical to his own publishing career. In 1844, these men would lead in the publication of the Home Library in the New York Tribune, March 30, 1844. It's likely Poe knew of this new venture, which had been advertised when he wrote to Matthews. These were relationships integral to Poe's literary future, particularly because they were in charge of a "collection whose plan was to include COPY-RIGHT WORK OF AMERICAN AUTHORS, and new works of En-glish writers, to be published by mutual arrangement with them and for their benefit."

By February of 1845 Poe had turned into a supporter of "The Young Americans." In June of that year, the Broadway Journal saw its last days. Poe approached Duycinick and Matthews to purchase it and loan him $50. In 1845 Griswold loaned Poe $50 to keep it afloat, but in January 3, 1846 the Broadway Journal closed.

By July 1845 Poe puffed the work of Duycinick, Matthews and others in the group, including "Library of Choice Reading" and the "Library of American Books," which one could assume is very much like The Library 100, Good Reads and most major magazines and newspapers book review sections.

Nineteenth Century writers were not immune to holding political beliefs and often what they wrote was a reflection of those beliefs. Yet, we seldom see attributions to the political points of view of writers, that context was rarely if ever communicated directly. Though in ret-rospect, females who were forced to write anonymously for centuries, many literally began to come out with a very clear feminist voice. The surfacing of same sex intimacy was also prevalent.

Margaret Fuller, Transcendentalist, critic, editor, author, reporter and woman's rights activist, who went with Anne Lynch Botta to retrieve letters Poe wrote to Frances Sargent Osgood, supported women's rights and Transcendental positions and was accused of being manly by Poe and others. She's said to have had a Transcendental, Romantic relationship with Thoreau and Emerson, which has also been described as "theological and philosophical."

Nineteenth century women writers and poets, Louisa May Alcott, Julia Ward Howe, Grace Greenwood, Alice Cary, Catherine Sedgwick, Emily Dickenson, Lydia Maria Child, Margaret Fuller, Ann S. Stephens, Elizabeth Fries Ellet and more refused to accept the separate roles of women. Ellet as a feminist and supportive of coming to the aid of abolitionist Lydia Mott and women's rights leader, Elizabeth Cady Stanton was certainly in league with other literary females of that new era of suffrage: Ann S. Stephens, Elizabeth Oakes Smith and other women writers, playwriters, journalists were feminists, some social reformers, abolitionists, women rights advocates, who frequented Botta's literary soirees. Most sought Poe for publishing their work in the Broadway Journal, but when that ended, Poe's Literati in Godey's Lady's Book came out in 1846 excluding Ellet, at a time when Poe was no longer welcome at Anne C. Lynch Botta's literary soirees.

Some of the men attending Anne C. Botta Lynch soirees included Ralph Waldo Emerson, Walt Whitman, both Transcendentalists, Herman Melville a dark romanticist, starting out as a Transcendentalist, from there his political views leaned toward social reform. Edgar Allen Poe, a dark romanticist, was adamantly against the "ideal of a Jeffersonian Democracy, and Horace Greely, Editor of the New Yorker, was an abolitionist and Rufus Griswold was a conservative.

In *The House of Expanding Doors*, it's noted that Anne C. Lynch Botta was referred to as "our dear Lynchie." The Horace Greeley Collection of 1840-1872 cites Anne as a member of the Liberal Republican Party of 1872 who nominated Greely for President, who passed away before the election, but won the support of the Democratic Party against Ulysses S. Grant's second term victory.

Comparing 19th century realist writers with Romantic writers among the Literati of New York, Martin Schaffer refers to the sociologist, Schwonke, who wrote that *In the Rise and Fall of Antiutopia: Utopia, Gothic Romance, Dystopia* that "romanticism and political conservatism are a natural pairing as science and utopianism is on the other end of the spectrum."

In Maria Karafilis's book, *American Racial Dystopia*, she writes that "scholars often analyze the stories of Poe in terms of chattel slavery, abolition, and fears of miscegenation." Karafilis refers to Poe and Hawthorne's "anti-utopic visions in favor of a dystopic vision of white annihilation that ultimately and inevitably issues from racial violence." Poe's stories are depicted by scholars as consisting of "chattel slavery, abolition and of relationships, reproduction between people of different ethnic groups, especially when one is white." Examples given concerning Poe, in which blackness is included in his narratives: "The Black Cat," "A Descent into the Maelström," "Hop-Frog," "Ligeia," "The Murders in the Rue Morgue," and The Narrative of Arthur Gordon Pym."

In Poe's short story *The Masque of the Red Death*, 1842, the red death is fictious. What it refers to is western expansion and Indian removal. Karafilis's position is that the book is not just about a "disdain for the politics of empire," but as an "annihilation of white culture." At the time President Andrew Jackson was intent on the removal of Indians, making the country white, while Poe's story alluded to the dissolution of both white and red men during the conflict and the domination and seizure of land. The expansion West Karafilis wrote that "it also suggests the disease of expansion and westward movement threatens white culture itself."

Distinctions began to exist in Literature, between American realism and romanticism in the 19th Century: reality and reason vs. emotion and fantasy. Poe wrote on the dark side of Romanticism, mysterious, supernatural and often horrifying and realists like Elizabeth Oakes Smith, a popular member of the New York literati, was recognized for her realism in poetry. She faced the dilemma like other female authors, having no control over the money she made, because husbands controlled their wives' earnings before the 19th amendment was passed, and poetry was not a lucrative genre then. Poets Alice and Phoebe Cary and Maria White Lowell were feminists and abolitionists who wrote realistic poetry. The sisters had worked for Susan B. Anthony and Lowell was part of Margaret Fuller's clique. As time changed, the civil war, feminism and equal rights were instigators toward a realistic writing era. By the 1890s, women writers had come into their own after centuries of banishment.

Catharine Sedgwick, a member of the Knickerbocker group and also an attendee at Ann Lynch Botta's Literary Soirees, was known for her realistic, later classified as modernist, depictions of domestic and regional culture. As a single woman, she didn't fit into an era of separate spheres, being that the unacceptability of single women dating was frowned upon. Ellet was not supportive of single women dating. What Sedgwick articulated in her book, Married or Single, published in 1857, was more attuned to the 20th and 21st century freedoms for women.

Catharine also brought to light the realistic details of what it was like for middle class and poor working women in New York's antebellum society. She concurred with the positions of Christine Stansell, a 21st century historian of social, sexual and cultural history of American women and gender relations in that era, that women suffered "economic duress, homelessness, lack of work, abandonment, dependent children and high infant mortality."

Catherine injected the laboring-class into fiction writing, which was a departure from city-mysteries replete with fabricated melodrama, why...because the real drama being played out daily in New York was about tenement women, who were preyed upon by men and women working side by side with men in sweat factories, with no rights over their pay, their children, their homes, considering that the 19th amendment didn't pass until 1920.

This rather new "sentimental prose" caught on with Margaret Fuller, Ann Stephens and Elizabeth Oakes Smith, all frequent Bluestocking attendees at Lynch's soirees, who had read Sedgwick before. One male critique, William A. Jones, referred to them as a "tribe of old women and "hangers-on in a cabal at aesthetic tea conversations and literary soirees."

Another contribution by Sedgwick was her success in "turning the novel of manners to American matter, in modifying the form for laboring-class readers, which likely helped to provoke James Fenimore Cooper's reactionary novels," such as *Home as Found* and *The Redskins*, books that elevated both "landed gentry (noble, upper class) and guarantee the civility and stability of the American social formation and polity (politically, societally organized)." Sedgwick was not included in men's club circuits, but nevertheless she inserted herself into "interactions with others and in ways that the Knickerbockers' mutual promotions involved her in more."

The popularity of female writers and public awareness grew during this period which was noticed by Edgar Allen Poe and critique William A. Jones, who went about applying their influence to out-maneuvering the Bluestocking ladies, in order to take control of the "American literary culture," resulting in women's contributions being understudied.

There appears to have been a concerted effort to control a Literary era by both New England critics, Poe and critics representing narrowly conservative positions, however there were also members of a group that was said to have approached criticism from a liberal, democratic viewpoint. Jones was a man Poe referred to as "our most analytic, if not best critic," but in Jones's assessment of the Bluestocking ladies, Poe's endorsement belies what appeared to be Jones's illiberal references to the female Literati.

Dime Novels, Historical Realism, Literary Realism, Women Write History

Considered a sub-genre of Women's Fiction, the Dime Novel craze of 19th Century America, was popular with writers as a medium to reach more readers, including Elizabeth Fries Ellet, Ann S. Stephens, referred to as a founder of Dime Novels, also including Louisa May Alcott, Henry Wordsworth Longfellow, Robert Louis Stevenson and even English poet Alfred, Lord Tennyson, who published their work in Dime Novels. Even Edgar Allan Poe created the "Gotham Letters" for the "Columbia Spy," which was intended for working class New Yorkers.

At the time Dime Novels were adventurous, often romanticized stories, many based on historical events, like the Revolutionary War, the Wild West of James Fenimore Cooper's Leather Stocking Tales. As Dime Novels went public around the time of the Civil War, the stories were fictionalized, historical retellings of events and their effects on a divided America. American realism began in the 1830s, becoming popular after the Civil War, while Literary Realism is a genre that was a reaction to Romanticism and a growing middle-class.

Historical Realism

Historical Realism is considered a new genre. Wikipedia describes Historical realism as a writing style or subgenre or realistic fiction centered on historical events and periods, which would classify some Dime Novels as Historical Realism.

Literary Realist

The Literary Realist movement initially occurred in the 1850s in France, and migrated all over Europe and America, over one hundred and fifty years ago. While Poe, a dark romanticist, is known today for his poetry, Gothic horror and detective stories and Osgood as a Romanticist, neither were realist writers, but Poe created Gotham Letters to the Columbia Spy focused on everyday life and was intended for mass readership. It's not too far-fetched to consider that a bevy of 19th century writers of both fiction and non-fiction, rejected romanticism for realism, as writers adapted to the growing public consumption, with a more educated middle class, by endeavoring to meet the challenge and rewards of writing for a mass audience with a new commercial vehicle. Ellet's Dime Novels were both romance fiction and historical realism.

Literary Realism was a 19th century literary movement based on "objective reality, with its focus on showing everyday activities in life, in identifying with the middle and lower-class society, without romantic idealization or dramatization." Granted the bulk of Dime Novels were overly dramatized, and categorized as a sub-genre of woman's fiction, a selling point for a female audience when it came to romance, but when it came to capturing the male audience, salability was in Wild West and Civil War topics, violence.

Real historical figures like Washington and Grant were popular and historical realistic events like stories of the Civil War were a hit in Dime Novels during the Civil War. In 1877, Beadle and Adams came out with the half-dime novel and there was also a nickel novel with the intent of bringing affordable reading to everyone. Typically, realist stories reflected ordinary people's daily lives, expressing all their human characteristics.

What sold for pennies on the dollar, Anne S. Stephens, a friend of Ellet's, also involved in defending Charlotte Meyers Griswold in a divorce case with Griswold, is also known for her contribution to Dime Novels and especially her Dime Novel western *Malaeska, the*

*Indian Wife of the White Hunter, New York: Irwin P. Beadle & Co.,
1860, which was listed on Sotheby for $3,000 recently.*

Ann S. Stephens

Ann, a feminist, is credited as the originator of the Dime Novel. Ann
and Elizabeth were friends, both writing Dime Novels and defending
the women involved in Griswold's duplicitous romantic proposals and
working as editors for the New York Evening Express. Ann was also
associate editor of the *Ladies Companion* magazine.

Anne S. Stephens

Ninety percent of Americans were literate in the era of Dime Novels, in consideration of the nominal cost, the working middle class could now afford books, increasing sales exponentially. While the themes were more suited to relatable topics for women, with a starting readership from women, who bought Ann S. Stephens's and Elizabeth Fries Ellet's Dime novels, the Civil War extended Dime Novel's popularity to men and topics changing to meet a male demographic, while some female writers adapted to western adventures.

In Poe On The Beat: Doings of Gotham As Urban, Penny Press Journalism, by Linda Patterson Miller, Poe's preference was to be a *magazinist*, not a newspaper writer. Poe became an urban contributor to the Columbia Spy in 1844 to publish a weekly correspondence from New York. Poe wrote real-to-life observations with a human perspective and the kind of enhancements atypical of Poe in rendering the scenes of New York's "glamour, intrigue and skullduggery with a human-interest focus, which scholars have said epitomized the penny press."

Poe's "Gotham Letters" for the "Columbia Spy," targeted working-class New Yorkers, who were considered to be losing ground in a city of merchants and professionals.

A fascinating aspect of the times was the developing technology to capture realism in the Daguerreotype and the use of real images in newspapers and magazines, which ultimately translated to realism, that knowledge and truth were non-symbolic.

Imagining Poe, considered one of the darker themed writers in history, writing about poverty in the New York City in the 19th Century, we'd expect a derisive tone. Poe wrote, "The "prevalent shanties of the Irish squatter, look like "tabernacles"; and a typical immigrant abode "nine feet by six, with a pigsty applied externally, by way of both portico and support. The whole fabric which is of mud has been erected in somewhat too obvious an imitation of the Tower of Piza." If Poe is writing for the class of people who likely could barely afford to read the Penny Press, how is this depiction helpful? He could have written about the Five Points, a New York slum, also "credited with creating tap dancing and hosting the prize-fight of the century, as well as welcoming visitors like Charles Dickens and Abrahm Lincoln." But he didn't. He likely just stuck to dark themes.

Though the Penny Press and the Dime Novel are "short, easy to carry and pass around," they have been compared to newspapers, but only the Penny Press, in contrast to regular papers, focused on news, not opinions and were less expensive, not to say that opinions were exempt. Dime Novels were most often fiction, though many were based on historical events, like the Civil War.

Ellet's Dime Novel focus was mainly romantic stories published in the Fireside Press, Beadles and Adams, The Waverly Library and weeklies like The Banner Weekly, The New York Weekly and the Saturday Journal.

Dime Novel Images

Dime Novel, penny press, became user friendly and accessible reads to thousands of America's working class, who were getting an education and for the first time interested in the news and reading newspapers. Ellet wrote and even Poe published in Dime Novels, in what became a lucrative option for writers.

Ellet story published in a dime novel

Elizabeth Ellet's Dime Novels

- *Love in a Maze, the Debutante's Disenchantment, Beadle and Adams, Fireside Library*
- *A Woman's World or the Adventures of a Young a Girl, Beadle and Adams, Fireside Library*
- *A Romance of a Poor Young Girl, Beadle and Adams, Fireside Library*
- *Love in a Maze, the Debutante's Disenchantment, Beadle and Adams*

- *Lady Helen's Vow or The Mother's Secret: A Romance of Love and Honor, Beadle and Adams, Fireside Library and Waverly Library*

Women Write History

In the 19th century Ellet's writing of history was not an acceptable genre for women, but she was also only writing exclusively about women, which broke another barrier. One must ask, why there was such opposition to Ellet writing history when historically there were at least twenty-five women who wrote history, other than Ellet. Women were writing history during the Revolutionary War. Why didn't Rufus Wilmot Griswold, anthologist, editor, poet, historian and critic, and William Gilmore Simms, poet, novelist, politician, historian, both, know that? Instead, they vehemently criticized Ellet for not giving them enough credit for their help in locating sources and made-it-known, that she was treading in male only territory. Why didn't they know she wasn't? If they were both here today, I'd give them a talking to, as if I am Mrs. Ellet, with sentiments phrased in terms of 21st century thinking and science, females have long been undercut by male domination, but here are examples that show, we always had it in us!

"In American Female Historians in Context," by Katherine Kish Sklar, whose focus was female historians and the variety of mediums they used to reach a female audience, books, Dime Novels, magazines, Elizabeth Fries Ellet was not the only female historian, but she is the only one to write about the American Revolutionary War excluding men entirely, a distinction which has awarded her significant attention and praise.

In Sklar's book, she outlines the three periods in which women wrote history, those born before 1800, those born between 1800 and 1850 and those born after 1850. The first group was defining history within the context of their local communities.

The second group wrote about everything that occurred within the context of both the Victorian literary world and newer local occurrences in a changing society, including "analytic and fictive writing." The third and last group were most often in pursuit of academic careers.

In "The lives and careers of the twenty-six women listed as "Historians" contained in "Notable American Women, a Biographical Dictionary," edited by Edward James, Janet James, and Paul Boyer, according to Katherine Kish Sklar, it is the most systematic sample of earlier female historians from 1770 to 1930. Considering, during Ellet's era, Griswold and others professed history was not the literary domain of women, which is another example, not just of historical inaccuracy, but an overwhelming period of male dominance, considering it has been documented the women had been writing history since the Revolutionary War.

From a list of twenty-six women, including Elizabeth Ellet, (1818- 1877), Mercy Otis Warren (1728-1814) to Frances Victor's (1826 to 1902) realistic novels to Clara Waters, (1834-1916) who wrote for Beadle's Dime Novels with "politely feminist" interpretations of the lives of women painters and biblical heroines, to Elizabeth Ellet's Practical Housekeeper, to name one book out of many books with an historical female focus, including *The Women of The American Revolution* series. Ellet (1912-18-1877) wrote exclusively about women, after years of "active literary effort."

Mercy Otis Warren

A feminist, politician, from a political family and historian living during the Revolutionary War, who Ellet included in her book *The Women of the American Revolution.* Mercy was told by one of our Founding Fathers that women shouldn't interfere in the male domain of politics.

Mercy Otis Warren

Most female historians were teachers, very few were economically independent, but all were aware of gender discrimination. Hannah Adams (1755-1831) was author of the first historical publication. In her memoir published in 1832, she wrote, "I was pressed by necessity to make every exertion in my power for my immediate support. During the American Revolutionary War, I learned to weave bobbin lace, which was then saleable, and much more profitable to me than spinning, sewing, or knitting, which had previously been my employment...."

Hannah Adams is known to have exemplified the less combative side of our American History during the early American period of female history writing, while Mercy Otis Warren (1728-1814, who was included in Ellet's book, *The Women of the American Revolution*, faced the conflicts that arose head on without hesitation, exerting herself in such a way, that she was immediately reminded of her proper place by one of our Founding Fathers.

In the mid-1770s, Mercy Otis Warren, living in Boston, where her father was a justice of the peace, her husband a member of the Massachusetts legislature, and her brother, all opposed to British policy, turned her parlor into a meeting place, with John and Samuel Adams and those opposed to royal policy, the British "writs of assistance," in attendance. Warren was to the left of Federalists like John Adams who opposed social revolution, and wrote a response in 1788 in a pamphlet, "Observations of the Constitution." In 1791 she defended the French Revolution, and in 1800 she supported Thomas Jefferson, enraging Federalist Boston. In 1805, her publication *History of the Rise, Progress and Termination of the American Revolution* (in three volumes) she accused John Adams, a founding father, of holding on to Monarchical beliefs. Warren put it this way, "Unfortunately for himself and his country he became so enamored with the British Constitution and the government, manners, and laws of the nation, that a partiality for monarchy appeared, which was inconsistent with his former professions of republicanism." Adams responded to Warren, demanding to know the basis of such allegations.

It appeared Adams' response was to refute her assessment by stating Warren must have known he was joking. But Warren responded by quoting him, "We are like other people, and shall do like other nations, where all well-regulated governments are monarchic." There were other occasions, Adams made "monarchial assertions," that Warren remembered, "I well remember my own reply," she wrote: "That a limited monarchy might be the best government, but that it would be long before Americans would be reconciled to the idea of a king."

The knowledge of this occurrence between a political astute woman and a founding father the from 1770s, got tossed into an historical vacuum. And what more appropriate time to bring it up before what will be a historical election in 2024 with a monarchal candidate, still in the running as I write.

It's possible that Ellet knew of Warren, her participation in the politics of the Founding Fathers, and that knowledge may have motivated her to write about the American Revolution by stepping into territory no woman had ever trespassed, Ellet writing about only women's contributions, with any mention of men, not even George Washington, but this likely feminist woman, Mercy Otis Warren was included in Ellet's "The Women of the American Revolution."

Warren was a female surrounded by a political family, immersed in the politics of the day, in the green days of our nation, exemplifying just another historical indication of separate spheres, unsurprisingly within our own government during its founding stages.

In response to Warren's politicking, Adams wrote "ten long letters of accusation and reproach, letters covering almost one hundred and fifty printed pages, later published by the Massachusetts Historical Society, in which Adams responded, declaring his hostility toward and fear of American Female Historians' History." Adams wrote that "History is not the Province of the Ladies." His finale to Warren "he was blushed by unfeminine willingness to discuss obscure matters of moral meaning." And her response to him: "Blush for yourself." Consider, not unlike the days of our founding fathers, feminine was not in any way comparable to feminist. Warren was a pioneer for women's rights; in that she demanded an equal voice for all women.

Within the context of Literary Genres, Ellet wrote about the history of women in all their endeavors, whether they were professional or domestic. Ellet's writing also fits into the categories of Literary Realism, Poetry, Early American Nature Writer, Children's writing and her own work and the work of others with translations in French, Italian, German and Spanish.

The Women of the American Revolution I, II, III
Domestic History of the American Woman
Pioneer Women of the West
Women Artists in all Ages and Countries
Queens of American Society
Rambles About the Country, A children's Non-Fiction Book
The New Cyclopedia of Domestic Economy, and Practical
    Housekeeper
The Eminent and Heroic Women of America
Summer Rambles in the West
Teresa Contarini

Ellet's "Rambles about the Country" (1840) a non-fiction, children's book, which Ellet has not received much credit for, was initially used as a text book in the Massachusetts School System, to introduce the varying landscapes and people living in parts of the country, with dissimilar landscapes, customs and ethnicity. Published by Popular Juvenile Works, Harper Brothers, the book was sold by many distributors for $1.20 and.35 cents and was included in Harpers Family Library. Written for children, including poetry, descriptive writing about place and people and historical writing about nature and parts of the country where Black Americans, were slaves, providing an all-encompassing look at the nation in the 19th Century.

In the chapter, "A Spring Day's Ramble," Ellet mentions race, which is the only time in her writing that she discusses the treatment of black people. Her audience is school children, many living in non-slave states. In the book, she argues slaves must be treated humanely. She wrote, "The poorer class of white people, at the South, are very badly off, for the comforts of life. The household and field labor being entirely performed by blacks, because it is looked upon as degrading to a white man or woman...and between the negroes and these people, almost a natural enmity seems to exist. The blacks, however, have greatly the superiority, in respect to comfortable food and clothing."

In the chapter, "The Legend of Lake Pepin," Ellet wrote, "I am conscious that I can point out to you but a very few of the curious and beautiful things you may see, in such a ramble. All must look for themselves; and, if you use your eyes to good purpose, during a short walk of an hour, you will never fail to find enough, largely to repay your attention."

As if she was speaking directly to us, in current 21st century vernacular, Ellet writes in the chapter "The Hawk's Nest &c.," (be mindful the book was first published as juvenile series book), "Have you ever observed, how much our own feelings operate on views of Nature?" She continues with, "Thus, the storms, which in a cheerful mood we would call magnificent, will, at another time, appear terrific. We cannot always take delight in the same scenes; but the beneficent Author of our being has formed us capable of varied enjoyment. To all frames on mind, can Nature minister delight. She has, for lighthearted youth, a smile an "a voice of gladness;" and for sorrow, "a mild and gentle sympathy." Then Ellet follows by inserting the Italian poet Pindemonte's poem, (a poem Ellet translated) who describes how two young ladies saw it.

Turn the page and Ellet writes, "I cannot describe to you the Hawk's Nest from my own impressions, having never visited the spot; but you shall have the description given to me by one or two intelligent young friends." Ellet employs a find and seek stratagem, even popular today in kids' books, setting to memory the footslog of others, and transcribing it into descriptive prose. Ellet wrote, "the way is past massive rocks that led to the great Kenhawa River. On both sides of you, the sun shines upon airy peaks, and forest-crowned hills, that shoulder each other, as far as the eye can reach, filling up the whole picture. They hem in the river, which is yet frequently seen, like a streak of snow, deep in the green bosom of the glen. Opposite of the place where you stand, is a frowning battlement of rock, looking like some ancient fortress or Gothic castle. It is vulgarly referred to as Hawks Nest, because the beetling ledge of rocks affords under it a place of shelter for birds of various kinds." Ellet said "some travelers think the Hawk's Nest, alone, is worth crossing the Atlantic to see"

In the chapter "Christmas in the Parishes," Ellet writes, "Will you take a peep at a Christmas, on a plantation?" Ellet refers to the Plantation as a "Kingdom in itself," with "sable" laborers who "may be termed the subjects, who all owe allegiance to their common sovereign, the master, who is amenable to the laws of his country, and to the opinion of society, for the manner in which he exercises his authority." In the same chapter she refers to black people as negroes and Blacks and how many of them are "industrious growing their own gardens, raising poultry, diving up eggs and chicken to their mistresses, some sold in town."

Ellet also describes scenes of "slave children who are joyous and careless with no anxieties, no sorrows, without the least exertion, like wiping their own mouths after an ordinary meal," but as "they grow older they're assigned to tasks, suited to their capacities, such as scaring crows from crops." And "older blacks weed the garden and sweep the spaces before doors and the older women with brooms in their hands," Ellet continued writing, "might have been caught and burned as witches, if they had happened to live in the old superstitious times."

For a white Christian woman, Ellet understood that their superstitions, charms, visions and "direful omens" were all founded in their traditions.

Ellet's perceptions are representative of a singular Southern plantation and are not representative of the treatment of slaves everywhere in the South and at other plantations. She added a derisive opinion that all "negroes are not industrious and that they're naturally the most indolent and improvident creatures on earth." That she believed this at all, and then put it in a book for children living in a non-slave state is unseemly. Also, when you consider she worked with Lydia Mott and wrote her letters during the civil war. Mott, who was the leader of the anti-slavery movement and conductor of the Underground Railroad, you have to wonder when or if Ellet changed her views?

Lydia Mott

Contents of Ellet's Letter to Lydia Mott, abolitionist and conductor of the Underground Railroad. Lydia, who worked with Elizabeth Cady Stanton and Anthony. Ellet mentions Susan B, Anthony and newspaper articles. Ellet inquiry was for a Mrs. Williams to inquire of Mr. Joseph Carey and Miss Mary Carey of their where abouts and what was known of Mrs. Williams' affairs. Ellet also mentions Mr. Dayton. The date is 1861. Ellet was acquainted with William Lewis Dayton, a lawyer and a Senator. Lydia was Lucretia Mott's cousin.

Lydia Mott letter

Rambles About the Country was published in 1847, Massachusetts was the first to abolish slavery outright, by judicial decree in 1783. In 1828, New York abolished slavery outright. The Civil War began in 1861, so though Ellet doesn't mention the state, we can assume it was any one of the Southern states that still allowed slavery. Ellet lived in South Carolina with her husband, before moving to New York, so she had to be familiar with the laws. Ellet's defense of women and her understanding of laws evidently did include slavery laws. In the 1800s slaves had no constitutional rights; they could not leave the plantations without permission, and with no control over their person hood, slaves could be "rented out, used as prizes in lotteries, or as wagers in card games or horse races." Treated as they were, it's not surprising plantation slaves lacked initiative as Ellet asserted.

Chapter 11

Commercialization, Politicization, Industrialization's Impacts on Spheres

In Separate Spheres, Female Worlds, Woman's Place: The Rhetoric of Women's History Author(s): Linda K. Kerber, published in 1988, we're seeing a timeline of perspectives on the separate spheres that existed between women and men, starting with Tocqueville.

Evidently when historians took on the task of looking into women's history, they turned to Tocqueville, the Frenchman who visited America in 1831. He was specifically looking at male and female spheres in his book, *Influence of Democracy on Manners Properly So Called.*

What Tocqueville described were different spheres, with marriage and the public opinion circumventing women's freedom within a "limiting boundary of choices," exactly what Ellet and women of that era found suffocating. Though women were defined as captives, Tocqueville considered them, as compared to other countries, as the "growing strength of the [American] people and ought to be attributed, I should reply: To the superiority of women."

In time, more than a half century later, after Tocqueville's visit, as we know, commercialization, politicization, industrialization changed the patriarchal culture, including separate spheres, but when we flash forward to the 21st Century, we see a complex set of spheres still.

In, 2023 female breadwinners tripled, often making more money than their husbands, but though women worked more, a 2023 Pew Study found women take on more of the bulk of work at home, which also applies to childcare.

It's fascinating that *The Women of the American Revolution*, Ellet's hallmark treatise on women's contributions may have contributed to enlightening women, giving them their first version through a female writer's retelling of the real-to-life experiences of women during the war, including politics, independence and "guerrilla" warfare. Domesticity was not their only calling, when needed, they too defended the country they hoped to secure as a homeland.

Kerber tracks us thru each defining period of change including *The Bonds of Womanhood*, by Nancy E Cott, who explains that the feminist political movement of the 19th Century found its voice because of separate spheres and created a feminist political movement in the nineteenth century that affected patriarchal control that resulted in the 19th amendment.

In *Up from the Pedestal* by Aileen Kraditor, written in 1968, Aileen wrote that the men's sphere was "the world and all its activities," proposing that the separation of the spheres was aligned with the Industrial Revolution, making clear distinctions between men and women in the sexual division of labor. In other words, men owned the world, women were still tethered to parameters men allowed within industry, domesticity and child care. Kraditor even referred to girls, women today, who are to a large extent expected to be responsible for childcare and have lost out on years of both educational and work opportunities. If, as Kraditor suggests, childcare was a shared responsibility, it would free women from the separate sphere's mentality that's existed for millennia. We see more shared responsibility of childcare today, but as a Pew Study attests, it's far from equal.

Aileen cites male bias in historians, women never gaining the same respectability as men in regard to their place in historical literature, which resulted in "bibliographies appended to books that deal with the time in which these women affected history." Concerning the current women's separation from spheres, which still exist, nevertheless women are attaining college degrees, with higher grades than men, better paying professions and relinquishing the idea that the tradition of home and children are necessarily a given.

Spheres are extremely apparent in the current political dynamics in a clash of positions, one adhering to a sphere's mentality, the other frees women to make their own choices. This is evidenced by rhetoric from Republican Senator Josh Hawley's book, *Manhood, the Masculine Virtues America Needs,* which has been assessed by every news outlet. Hawley suggests men are under attack. Though I've never read his book, I've heard about it, so my take is what he is actually talking about is spheres, a preference to return to the 19th century or earlier, where woman's roles were limited to house, housework and childcare. Data shows men are working less, watching more porn and having health issues. Evidently, Hawley blames this on liberals who he says wants to abolish masculinity. His party is removing women's reproductive rights, but instead of talking about what's really at issue, is that the Republican Party's "War on Women," via their policies and legislation, is the spheres battle of the 21st century.

Gerda Lerner, *In the Lady and the Mill Girl*, contends that "American Industrialization" took place when the economy necessitated female and child labor, which ultimately revealed dissimilarities in class and social attitudes. The dynamic changed when working women left their homes, while stay-at-home women had an elevated status per spheres. The saying "Women's Place is in the Home," the "Cult of True Womanhood" was elevated by middle class women elevating their own status.

The Retail Revolution, the commercialization of America in the 19th century would not have occurred without female factory workers. Clothing normally hand sown at home was now being manufactured, but not by upper-class women. They were looking at magazines like Godey's Lady's Book and ordering all the new styles from department stores. In New York there was A.T. Stewart in 1846, Lord and Taylor in 1826, originally dry goods only, and Macy's in 1851, also a dry goods store turning into a commercial retail venture.

The commercialization of goods contributed to the rise of Capitalism and middle-class females had an integral role, both manufacturing, selling and wearing fashions that fit their lifestyles, thus bettering their statures and ameliorating the male grip. The Married Women's Property Acts of 1860, devised state by state, allowed married women to handle their own earnings and property.

The driving commercial force of women in manufacturing and the marketplace allowed them to extend their power beyond male, female spheres, that women can do this, beyond male dominant control. All these changing societal elements particularly emboldened females, who could not own property, nor vote, nor have legal rights to their off-spring, nor work outside the home and were controlled by their husbands, which would include mostly middle-and upper-class females. Considering this over 150 years later, it's understandable, that many men who lived in Ellet's circle in particular, would oppose any interference, thus calling her derogatory names to defame her.

Fast-forward to today, women are more supportive of reproductive rights and equal rights than men. The wage gap still exists, and if you ask what the biggest problems are women face today, it's patriarchy, a word Hawley likely failed to use in his book, despite the fact, that is the crux of the problem with men in the 21st and similar to the 19th century, with Poe, Griswold and likely most men.

Ellet's pro-female defense, her contention that Osgood's reputation was being harmed, Ellet's defense of Griswold's second wife in contrast to Griswold's polygamist attempts, and all her other defenses of women mentioned in this book countermand the Poe Society's accusations that Ellet's concern for Osgood was due to Ellet's own romantic interest in Poe. What she wanted were good reviews and publication, which materialized regardless of Poe, but over 150 years later, there's now a potpourri of Poe plots against her, like one blog that says Poe was having an affair with both Osgood and Ellet. When one considers that era isn't much different from our own, we're still titillated by romantic who-did-its, just check out almost every magazine and tabloid, so this is likely one of Poe's greatest successes via his Foundation and Society, the only out-standing problem is where's the evidence of this pursuit over 150 years later? Again, it's likely that's why Ellet's autograph album was purchased by a Poe Society blogger Kelly Keener.

Griswold was Osgood's literary agent. In 1849 Griswold warned Ellet to stop gossiping about Osgood and Poe. *In Thy Named Concealed: Frances Osgood's Poems on Parting with Edgar Allen Poe,* by Mary De Jong, she wrote that though Griswold was devoted to Osgood, we also know he was emotionally involved with another woman, namely Alice Cary. And then there's the other women he was courting. We could refer to Griswold as a serial womanizer…his efforts to silence Ellet were solely an act to protect Osgood. After her death, he wrote, "Fanny's spirit looks down on me as I write." What De Jong referred to as third parties, who learned of Poe's and Osgood's correspondences, convinced Osgood "to protect her reputation, by recalling her letters." This angered Poe and further alienated him from the literary establishment, as described by De Jong, which is an entirely different interpretation out-of-the-mouth of Rufus Griswold, who also enamored with Osgood.

Ellet's reveals, supported by her contemporaries Margaret Fuller and Anne C. Stephen, concerning a woman she perceived to be in a situation that could harm her reputation, didn't go unnoticed. Because of her actions and writings which captured the roles of women invariably countermanded by 19th Century male dominance, she was contacted by the most famous female abolitionists in American history, Elizabeth Cady Stanton and Susan B. Anthony. After Ellet published the three volumes of *Women of the American Revolution*, 1848 to 1850, is when Stanton called for women's suffrage in Seneca Falls, New York. In the 1850s Stanton supported liberalized divorce for women, even pietistic women of the temperance movement.

What we know from footnotes in papers of Elizabeth Cady Stanton and Susan B. Anthony is that Anthony herself contacted Ellet for assistance in 1860 when a woman fleeing her abusive husband sought asylum in New York for herself and her daughter. Anthony wrote about the case in a letter to Stanton. Ellet helped conceal the fugitives. What this says about Ellet is that she was not just a literary maven, she was in touch with American women's rights advocates of the time in her defense of women, both in her writing and in life.

The knowledge of Ellet assisting a woman and her child fleeing an abusive husband is important in understanding Ellet's response to the behavior of both Poe and Griswold, which was to protect the woman involved. It's likely that Stanton and Anthony heard of the events involving Poe and Osgood, Griswold and his divorce case, and Ellet's involvement. Not only did Poe and Griswold compete when it came to who was the superior literary genius, but both were also romantically attracted to Frances Sargent Osgood. The consequence was Ellet interceded in both Poe and Griswold's 19th-century approach of dismissing their behavior as inconsequential to the reputations of women. Stanton's vision was to unleash women from the male domination of keeping women at home, housekeeping, and parenting with few of their own rights as was indicated in the restrictions of the "Cult of Domesticity."

In the 1840s, the passage of Married Women's Property Acts in Ellet's home state of New York was enacted in April of 1848, about three months before the Seneca Falls Convention. The passing of the Acts "put married women on an equal footing with their husbands related to contracts, earnings, ownership of property and the right to sue or be sued." These occurrences likely had an impact on Ellet's already apparent sense of the importance of women's equality.

The disparagement of Ellet by Poe even continues to this day. One would think that 19th century standards for men and women don't hold true today; didn't the Women's Voting Rights Act and the 21st-century Me Too movement contribute to change? How much change…careers and lives are similarly impacted today by differences in male, female societal conduct and treatment. It's likely that if Poe, Osgood, and Ellet were alive today, you'd read about them in *People* magazine. Infidelity and gossip did not remain just a 19th-century intrigue.

The anonymous sale of Ellet's autograph album in 2015 did not just reemerge in the fall of 2015, as Kelly Keener, who has volunteered and written articles for the Poe Society, stated. She also stated there was an anonymous sale of the album, eventually admitting the Poe Society bought the album. Their objective was to reveal letters they feel vindicate Poe, further incriminate Ellet. There is ample evidence that other members of the "Literati of New York," also expressed their concern for Osgood's reputation. History will remember Poe's genius, but they'll also remember his separate spheres mindset, not dissimilar to men today.

Chapter 12

Ellet and Maggie Fox, The Love Life of Dr. Kane, Spiritualism and Social Change

Ellet Letter to Maggie Fox Kane

Ellet writes Maggie Fox inquiring if she was alright and her whereabouts. The trials and tribulations Maggie suffered due to the consequences of her secret love affair, Elijah Kane's refusal to publicize their relationship and his family's refusal to a accept their marriage and provide her with a dowry to help support her.

Margaret Fox Kane

Dear Maggie

Since I heard through the news-papers of your return to the spiritrapping profession (for which I never blamed you) I have not been able to learn your address. Kate never answers a note, and is never at home. and Mrs Bayard did not know your whereabouts. Will you let me know where you are, and what you are doing? I shall be here till 1st Sept. I have some suggestions to make. Write to me to the above address.

yours truly

Maggie Fox Kane letter

What is now recognized as the Modern Spiritualist movement which began in 1848, with the Fox sisters in upstate New York, it became a movement for social change, an alternative to Christianity. Elizabeth Lowry wrote in *Spiritual (R)evolution and the Turning of Tables: Abolition, Feminism, and the Rhetoric of Social Reform in the Antebellum Public Sphere*, that Margaret (Maggie) Fox Kane and her two sisters were initially known for "snapping" messages with a ghost who lived in a house they had moved into, which was rumored to be haunted.

Ellet had close contact with Margaret Fox Kane while helping her claim the dowry promised her by Elijah Kane. Margaret's spiritualist ties were deemed unacceptable to a wealthy family whose high society intolerance and religious beliefs forbade their relationship and denied they were married. Margaret's love affair of the letters with Elijah Kane was compiled by Ellet in the anonymous book, *The Love-Life of Dr. Kane.*

At the time Spiritualists were advocating for reforms that were deemed radical and violated the status quo. Spiritualist practices were used by the abolitionist movement and among feminists for the purpose of social reform. This coincided during a period when women had few rights, so spiritualism allowed women to speak publicly, thus airing the issues concerning women's rights. How the feminist movement correlates with Spiritualism is fascinating and likely not well understood or known. Certainly, to be a Spiritualist was not a well-accepted practice in the 19th Century.

In Spiritual (R) evolution and the Turning of Tables: Abolition, Feminism, and the Rhetoric of Social Reform in the Antebellum Public Sphere, Elizabeth Lowry provides the background we need to connect interrelated significant changes that brought about reforms, such as abolitionism, spiritualism, feminism and new social reforms, particularly for women.

It was 1850, Stanton and Anthony formed the first National Women's Rights Convention in Worcester, MA. That year the Fugitive

Slave Act was passed. That meant free states had to conform to authority's laws in Southern states, by handing over slaves who escaped, which resulted in political and economic instability. Also, with the addition of new scientific discoveries, petrol refining, color photography processing, dishwashers, sewing machines and new movements like abolitionism, spiritualism, feminism, social reforms disrupted the status quo and supplanted religious beliefs that upheld women's diminished standing, what they could and couldn't do. Spiritualist practices were a countervailing force against public spheres, functioning as an oppositional discourse according to Lowry.

What made spiritualism so popular in the 19th century when cultural norms were fixed and sacred, particularly for women? Lowry is very clear that Spiritualism was used in terms of speech and persuasion by abolitionists and feminists, challenging separate spheres, therefore establishing the viability of alternative beliefs and behaviors that were forbidden.

Unsurprisingly, it was the convergence of industrialization, railroad transportation and an intellectual, spiritual, and an emotional awakening that evolved, resulting in Americans of the 19th century embracing spirituality, even preferring it to Christianity. It was 1850 and the first Women's Rights Convention was held, the Fugitive Slave act was passed exacerbating dissension between blue and red states. Spiritualism broke the allegiance to Christianity in seeking reforms, including "abortion, free love and women's rights." As you can imagine, knowing our history, at that time, "conservatives" felt Spiritualism and politics could spark a revolution, which it did in 1861, when those differences resulted in a Civil War between Red and Blue states.

Flash-forward 2023, the 21st Century resurgence of this quasi-political-religious comeback, a movement to control/eliminate the freedoms of women, Black Americans, denying racial history, gender differences, forbidden in the 19th Century, was resurrected again in the name of what could be referred to as false-freedom in the 21st Century.

In the 19th Century "free love," meant an absence of legal ties and to freely choose to end a marriage. Considering women were contracted to their husbands legally when it came to almost all legal rights involving a marriage, it was a monumental transformation. Fast Forward to 2023 and no-fault divorces are now being considered in Congress and contested by Republicans, which is not radical in this century, because it simply gives either party the option of terminating a marriage based on no wrong doing.

By way of Thomas and Mary Nichols, in 1850, "free love" or the "anti-marriage theory" essentially permitted women the right to instigate relationships outside of marriage, allowing women the ability to do what men could always do. In "The "Anti-Marriage Theory" of Thomas and Mary Gove Nichols A Radical Critique of Monogamy in the 1850s" by Patricia Cline Cohen, no other women from the 1840s to 1850s supported "free love." Cohen wrote that Elizabeth Cady Stanton, who had a friendship with Gove, discontinued that amiability, despite the fact she upheld the position that marital relations subordinated women. Still, when the History of Woman Suffrage was published in 1880, there was a single section by Mary Gove Nichols, which credited her for being an early lecturer on women's health.

Deeper observations of the couple by Cohen revealed the seedier side of New York, also defining differences in their behavior, he was having extra-marital relations with the madams of New York's brothels, while she maintained the belief that wives could refuse sex with their spouses as well as having extra marital relations. Apart from their professional credits, he a journalist and medical doctor, she a woman's health advocate and women's physiology and anatomy lecturer, there were also life experiences that created their partnership and the reality of what a marriage certificate provided. Mary compared it to how a pass for slaves allowed black men their mobility. Incredibly, a marriage certificate precluded the threat of arrest for fornication, lewd behavior. Mary's belief was that "both slavery and marriage were bad institutions," but while they existed it was prudent to have a pass."

Marriage vs free love was interpreted by Spiritualists, in considerably more semi-religious terms, that "spiritual affinity was the basis of relationships in the beyond and sought just connections in the here and the now."

The Una was a feminist publication that like its audience insisted on marriage laws that included a divorce option. Elizabeth Cady Stanton called for divorce laws at the 1860's Women's Rights Convention. It wasn't until 1937, when the Matrimonial Causes Act, which followed decades of political pressure by women, who sought divorce on the same terms of men for the first time passed.

Spiritualism was considered Satanic by religious Christians, but 19th Century women refused to believe they and their children would be damned without a conversion. Spiritualism was construed as the political religion of Suffragettes. Lowery wrote that it was a disruption, a revolutionary change, seen as an immediate threat to patriarchal structures of that era. Concerning the 21st century period we're now living in, it's apparent we still face political and religious restrictions that similarly are about control, not freedom.

Ellet came to the aid of spiritualist Margaret, Maggie Fox Kane, to help her collect a dower, after learning of the secret marriage between Fox and Dr Elisha Kane and love letters Maggie possessed. In a Dissertation by David Alexander Chapin, University of New Hampshire, Durham, *exploring other worlds: Margaret Fox, Elisha Kane, and the antebellum culture of curiosity,* Chapin provides us with details about Ellet's intervention, in the affair of the letters between Margaret Maggie Fox, spiritualist and Dr Elisha Kane, the wealthy, famous Artic explorer who was concerned that a known romantic affiliation with Maggie, a spiritualist, could harm his reputation.

A lawyer Ellet contacted deemed that there was a "legally binding union under the Common Law and laws of New York State, which should have given Fox the rights of a widow." Because Margaret moved around from place to place, drank excessively and had no monetary assistance, Ellet's concern was to help Maggie, who wanted to publish the love letters to reveal the truth of their relationship, while the Kane family accused Ellet of wanting to write a book. The Lawyer's position was that he was "a friend, on behalf of a woman ignorant of her rights and laws of her country," which conveyed "there was time to settle, informally, quietly, or if necessary, through legal recourse, which would be public."

With the threat of disclosure Elisha Kane attempted to regain control of Maggie, remove her from her Spiritualist leanings. To counteract Ellet, a priest and friend of Dr. Kane, helped to end Maggie's practice of spiritualism and she became a Catholic and an adherent to the paternalistic order.

Dr. Kane claimed he was never married to Maggie Fox, due to her beliefs and social standing. It was all about Kane's position and reputation, which he felt would be damaged by aligning with a female spiritualist. Despite once denying a formalized tie, Kane had written they had been married. The letters had the potential to harm the family's prestige, thus Maggie Fox Kane became a victim of her love life with Dr. Kane. To make matters more complicated, she was dependent on him or the Kane family for support, but their intent was to disenfranchise her.

Ellet could have published those letters, which the Kane family would have ultimately fought, but it would hurt Dr. Kane's reputation, while the Fox relatives felt it was more than appropriate. Ultimately, Maggie was caught between competing interests, so, she kept the letters, and held back on releasing and publishing them. Obviously, the Kane family didn't appreciate Ellet's influence on Margaret, but there were no personally derisive remarks or attacks as compared to Poe and the continued defamatory and false attacks by Poe defenders.

Dr. Elisha Kane ultimately agreed to provide her with an increase in her income as long as her behavior was suitable. Instead, her isolation, drinking and concerning behavior contributed to her decline, and in 1862, she agreed to publish Elisha's letters. An arrangement was made with a New York publisher after Elisha Kane's death. Margaret hired a lawyer, but Robert Kane, Dr. Kane's brother, countersued, and the book did not go to the publisher. This occurred because Maggie was eventually given a specified allowance.

The agreement consisted of a stipulation, that if the payments stopped, the letters, no longer in Maggie's possession, would be returned to her. The letters were placed with Dr. Edward Bayard, who had previously attended to Maggie's health. In 1865, the payments stopped, and the letters were ultimately published in *The Love Life of Dr. Kane,* an anonymous book compiled by Elizabeth Fries Ellet, her name appearing nowhere, but, "according to primary sources in Elisha Kent Kane Papers, they clearly indicated Elizabeth Ellet's central role in the preparation of the volume."

As revealed In a Dissertation by David Alexander Chapin, University of New Hampshire, Durham, *Exploring other worlds: Margaret Fox, Elisha Kane, and the antebellum culture of curiosity,* this is what Ellet wrote, "Perhaps many will think that no circumstances could justify the publication of the letters contained in this volume," but, she continued, "Maggie Fox has borne the sneers of the world, and the neglect of those whose regard for the deceased should have induced them to protect, comfort, and befriend her. She had been slandered in the press and humiliated by the Kane family," said Ellet, "and she was finally denied the money left to her by Kane. To make matters worse, the papers were repeating the Kanes' claim that Maggie Fox had never married Elisha Kane. "Could any woman who respected herself, submit to such an indignity?" asked Ellet. "What was there about her whom Dr. Kane had wooed and wedded, that she should be thus insulted, and denied common justice under an outrageous imputation? Her sole means of defense," continued Ellet. "Her only vindication was the publication of this correspondence, Maggie Fox was a poor girl, who found herself being mistreated by the rich and powerful." Ellet asserted that the personal letters of Dr. Kane were being published as a last resort in defense of the defenseless. "The world usually sides with the rich, the proud, and the powerful; and it is not expected that the poor, the humble and the weak, will receive either justice or sympathy." Before the American public, however, the humble could attain justice. The private dispute between Margaret Fox and the Kane family was being presented to the public much as spirit-rapping had been. Let the public decide who was right and who was wrong."

Through the book, *The Love Life of Dr. Kane,* which was published posthumously, Ellet compiled the book to reveal who both Dr. Elisha Kane and Maggie Fox Kane were, allowing readers to come away with their own assumptions, but as the title conveys, the book's focus is on Dr. Elisha Kane.

Ellet wrote, "We are all the more touched by his tenderness and wonder at the depth and ardor of the love that impelled him."

In reference to Kane's heroic Arctic travels and his feelings for Maggie Fox, Ellet wrote, "So, the little incident of his carrying the portrait of his beloved one strapped to his back, through the dreary Arctic wastes, gives us a better insight into a true and noble heart than all the anecdotes collected by his biographer."

It was reported in The New York Times that "Margaret Fox was to be evicted from her tenement house in New York and a sympathetic spiritualist took her in, only to die on March 8th, 1893." Elizabeth Fries Ellet passed away in 1877.

Chapter 13

Lydia Mott, Women's Rights Advocate, Leader Anti-Slavery Movement, U.S. Civil War. Ellet assisting Elizabeth Packard, Women's Reformer, whose Husband Committed Her to An Asylum Over Disagreements and Safeguarding Phoebe Harris Phelps, Children's Book Author and Her Child's Flight from Her Abusive Husband

It was in 1852 that Susan B. Anthony, encouraged by Lydia Mott, decided to pursue the fight for women's rights. Ellet contacted Lydia in a letter at the start of the Civil War in 1861, that a Mrs. Williams directed by Stanton, had requested the whereabouts of Mr. Joseph Carey and Miss Mary Carey and what she might know about them. From 1861 to 1865 New York was involved in the Civil War. After South Carolina seceded in January of 1861, New York Mayor Wood suggested New York follow and secede January 7, 1861, which never happened. This indicates that Ellet's letter to Lydia Mott could be somehow related to that state of affairs at the time when The Fugitive Slave Act of 1850 prohibited interfering in the capture of slaves. Union states were not allowed to help blacks fleeing protection, which complicated the relationships between New York and the South. Not surprisingly New York's businesses had close ties to the South. Much of the South's cotton exports passed through New York, and the city's merchants profited from cotton, which translated to slavery, resulting in Broadway hotels and stores filled with customers, including new brownstones and construction everywhere.

Research is ongoing to determine who Mrs. Williams was and Joseph and Mary Carey were, whose last name is the same as the prominent New York Carey family.

Ellet's contact with Lydia in 1861 is another indication of her willingness to become more than a conduit, but an activist on behalf of people desperate for assistance, a propensity she repeated throughout her residency in New York. As a participant, Ellet became involved with Lydia Mott, and Abigail Hopper Gibbons, abolitionist and social welfare activist in supporting Elizabeth Packard, a New York socialite married to Minister Theophilus Packard. It's possible that Ellet hid Elizabeth Packard at the request of Elizabeth Cady Stanton after she illegally removed Parker from a mental asylum. Elizabeth Packard expressed views different from her husband, where religion was con-cerned, consequently, because women had no rights, men were prone to committing women who didn't obey them. In other words, women who did not abide by the separate sphere's rules of that era, who held their own opinions and ambitions, separate from their domestic duties and paternal oversight, was unacceptable to the degree that women could be committed, without any legal protections.

It's known that Lydia Mott, cousin of Lucretia Mott, feminist activist, Abolitionist, both working for suffrage, worked with women's rights leaders including organizing events, lobbying and communica-tions, and being the leader in the anti-slavery movement. Quaker Abo-litionist sisters, Abigail and Lydia Mott and their cousin, feminist and Abolitionist Lucretia Mott taught Rosetta Douglass when she was six. Rosetta, who was black, became an abolitionist and social reformer. Rosetta's father was Frederick Douglass, renowned reformer, Aboli-tionist and Suffragist.

From 1861 to 1865, New York, which was the most populace state in the Union, became a major source and supply route for not only weaponry but militia to the Federal Army. During this period Elizabeth Cady Stanton continued to fight for women's rights midst the contrasting anti-feminist Abolitionists, while she continued stressing the comparison between slavery and the suppression of all women.

The 15th Amendment was passed in 1865, and historians questioned whose rights were preeminent, the white educated women Stanton represented, or the black men who were captives? What remained questionable is why were black women excluded, was it just because they were women, which would indicate that spheres also precluded the emancipation of black women.

In Nancy Hoffman's *Teaching about Slavery, the Abolitionist Movement, and Women's Suffrage*, between 1830 and 1870, she writes, "it's a critical moment in time for the proper placement in time for black men and women and white women and their rights in American Society." What was also revealed was racial prejudice and the inequality of the sexes, which sadly persists today.

Depending on which historians' views you except for that period in our history, current or past, it's indicative of how past and present views are subjective, as they have always been, depending on differing viewpoints. *In The Feminized Civil War: Gender, Northern Popular Literature, and the Memory of the War, 1861-1900,* by Alice Fahs, it's interesting to note that Northern women's response to the Civil War was depicted as "exclusionary and restrictive nationalism" even though it was considered somewhat experiential, at the time, and not historical in comparison to the effect of the Revolutionary War. Fah's cites Ellet for celebrating Revolutionary woman, but due to what she describes as an "emergent masculinized and radicalized culture of the 19th century increasingly foreclosed the association of Northern women and African Americans with participation in the war."

The truth of what Fahs pointed out was there were two battles, "one way on the battle-front, and another "where a woman's war of sacrifice and suffering complemented a man's war of fighting." This would have been in the 1860s, and there was greater knowledge of the Civil war by women and a middle-income populace buying Dime Novels filled with fictionalized war-time stories. Interestingly, Fahs wrote, there was both feminized and masculinized war-time literature available.

During the Civil War, reformers in the Women's Movement refocused on the war effort, rather than organizing women's rights meetings. Louisa May Alcott, a feminist and a suffragist, she was a frequent guest at Lynch's literary soirees. She wrote a *Story of Experience,* about a female whose husband died in the war in 1873.

Sarah Josepha Hale, Lady's Godey's Magazine publisher, is known for trying to stop the Civil War. Hale, contrary to her employer, Louis Godey. In the 1860s, the magazine had a huge readership, both from the South and the North. "Hale wanted a Union, so she invented one, by writing articles in support of a united country and creating a "cover fiction" to unite women all over the country.

However, In *Reorienting "Lost" Time: Reading Godey's Lady's Book in the American Civil War*, by Charlotte Hand, we are reminded of Sarah Josepha Hale, publisher of Godey's Lady's Book, maintaining a separate spheres position. Which coincides with her disapproval of women associating with partisan politics, which ultimately included discussions of war, which are invariably political. Hale supported expanded women's spheres when it came to education and professional occupations, but not in politics. Comparing Godey's Lady's Book of the 19th century to Vanity Fair of 2024 as an example, the content has changed drastically, there are no longer women's magazines on fashion and home life that aren't spattered with political news, "culture, style and politics," in what still remains true is that women, both black and white women are still fighting for equality.

In 1861, Ellet could be described as betwixt and between the cult of true womanhood and feminism, although in Langer's reassessment of Ellet's work, she describes her in feminist terms and certainly Ellet's constant support of women is an indication of her sense that social responsibility, should include women, in that they were literally confined to a subservient lifestyle, confined to their homes, their male prescribed roles.

In a re-review of *Women Artists in all Ages and Countries,* by Sandra L. Langer, she apprises Ellet's work as feminist, thus requiring a feminist interpretation Ellet demonstrated over and over again, in her writing and her actions, exemplifying that women's rights issues were paramount to her.

In the case of Elizabeth Packard, whose Minister husband put her into an asylum about 1860, because she wouldn't abide by his religious tenants, Packard was removed from her home and children. Susan B. Anthony, after Packard's 18 months of incarceration, rescued her and hid her, refusing to reveal her where abouts. Abigail Hopper Gibbons, an abolitionist and social welfare activist, Lydia Mott, and Ellet pleaded with Anthony to release her, Anthony refused. Husbands owned everything, including their children, income, properties, and their wives. Just another indication how women were at their mercy, so Anthony went ahead and rescued Elizabeth Packard, an American rights advocate, who was separated from her children, and Ellet likely had something to do with giving her refuge.

We know that Ellet likely concealed more than one woman, but we know one particular instance, at the request of Susan B. Anthony who a woman and her daughter fleeing from her abusive husband was, Phoebe Harris Phelps, a successful children's book author. We know this from a letter Ellet sent, at about the time she had replaced Ann Stephens in 1857 as literary editor of the New York, Evening Press. The letter requested a pass for her and a female friend for passage on the New Jersey Central Rail from New York to Scranton, PA. Ellet wrote she would acknowledge the favor in any way in her power. The letter which is included in the index is from the David, McNeely Stauffer Papers, Manuscripts and Archive Division, NYPL Astor, Lenox, Tilden Foundations. The return address on the letter is WN Lummis &

Company, New York. WN Lummis, stands for William Nixon Lummis, her father, (1775–1833), in tribute to him and likely the address of her brother in New York.

Chapter 14

Feminists as Artists, Transcendentalists, New York Suffragettes, Suffragists

Elizabeth Cady Stanton and Susan B. Anthony, *The Una, The Lily, The Revolution* vs Sara J. Hale's *Godey's Lady's Book*

Lucretia Mott, feminist, advocate for ending slavery, supporting suffrage Susan B. Anthony and Elizabeth Cady Stanton, who cofounded the American Equal Rights Association, the 19th century's most renowned females dedicated to the rights of women.

In Women Artists of all Ages, Ellet defended the attire of Harriet Hosmer, an American sculptor who appeared in an engraving wearing a shorter dress with her bloomers showing. Ellet commented that she was definitely a female and not a man, after criticism of the sculptor's attire. When Nathaniel Hawthorne went to visit Hosmer in Rome, he was taken aback because she had no petticoats, questioning her femininity. Bloomers were introduced in 1848 and named after Amelia Jenks Bloomer. She was the first women to own, operate, and edit a newspaper for women called the Lily. Fuller edited the Transcendental periodical, The Dial at the invitation of Ralph Waldo Emerson.

Amelia Jenks Bloomer

Amelia was an early suffragist, a social activist and the editor of the *Lily*. She was a fashion advocate who updated women's clothing styles, which received much disapproval from 19th Century men.

Amelia Jenks Bloomer

In 1848 Amelia Bloomer attended the Seneca Falls Convention. In 1851, Bloomer introduced the suffragettes Elizabeth Cady Stanton and Susan B. Anthony to each other. Sarah Margaret Fuller, member of the Literate of New York, Editor for Horace Greeley's New York Tribune, friend of Ellet and Poe requested Poe return Osgood's letters with Anne Lynch Botta, both were among a group of women who supported Stanton and Anthony as women's rights activists, supporting Wollstonecraft's feminism and the Rights of Women.

At the Seneca Falls Declaration in 1848 the state of New York passed the Married Women's Property Law; this law became the template for other states to grant married women the right to own property.

The timeline related to how the women's rights events impacted the decision of Ellet, Fuller, Botta and others to protect Osgood's reputation and was likely attributable to their belief in the emerging feminist ideology, versus separate spheres male domination. It's not coincidental that on Ellet's trip west, she often mentioned the incivility, patriarchal behavior of men toward women in her book *Summer Rambles in the West.*

Though Ellet's participation in the feminist movement was less apparent in the public realm, possibly her own intent not to be categorized in a way that would distract from her readers' acceptance, particularly in Godey's Lady's Book, with more of a Cult of True Womanhood focus, rather than the new feminism women were adopting. Nevertheless, Ellet, in a less public way, was involved. In a footnote in the edited papers of Stanton and Anthony, Anthony turned to Ellet for assistance in 1860, when a woman fleeing her abusive husband sought asylum in New York for herself and her daughter. Ellet helped conceal the fugitives, and Anthony wrote of the sensationalized case in a letter to Stanton. There were two women that we know of who sought help from abusive husbands, but there were likely more incidents in an era when women had few rights.

Sarah Margaret Fuller

Philosopher, journalist, literary critic, feminist and Transendentalist, and the first female war correspondent, Fuller has aged well in that her contributions have endured more than many of her female contemporaries. Fuller eviscerated the 19th century do and don'ts that men demanded, which is why she is still so popular today, in view of 19th century similarities women share with her in the 21st century.

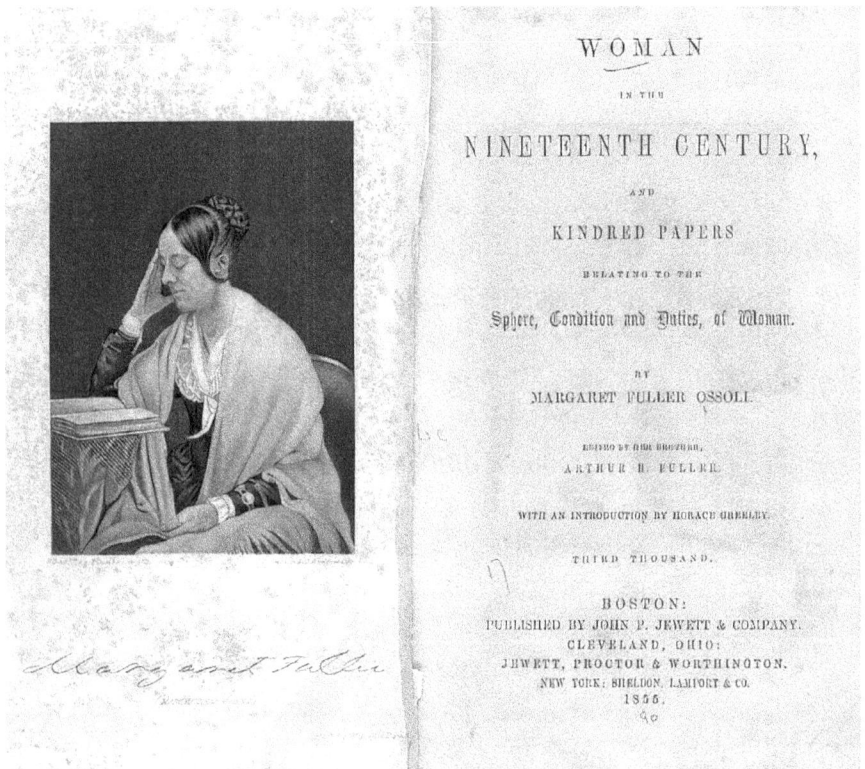

Margret Fuller photo inside *Women of the 19th century*

Margaret Fuller's *Women of the 19th century* appeared in 1845. In an unsigned series in the Broadway Journal in the same year, Fuller's vision of women's equal standing with men was disputed by Poe. He was the editor of the Broadway Journal from 1845 to 1846. The article stated that Fuller's positions opposed the laws of Nature, experience, and revelation. Fuller's literary accomplishments and her book were denounced on the premise that the writing style, clarity, somehow reflected badly on its premise, which was female equality, that "she could not compose a logical treatise." Fuller also spoke to the anti-slavery female speakers of her day that reached out to audiences in ways men could not when speaking to anti-slavery. Stanton, Anthony and Sojourner Truth wanted women included in amendments with equal protections under the law, but the 14th amendment which protected equal protection under the law included only the word "male" into the Constitution for the first time.

In 1848, three hundred women and men met for the Women's Rights Movement in Seneca Falls on behalf of women who were prohibited from the rights and privileges of men, white and black.

When the 15th amendment passed in 1869 giving Black Men the right to vote on the basis of race Stanton and Anthony, who were both Abolitionist, were opposed because it didn't include women, black and white.

In *White Suffragist Dis/Entitlement: The Revolution and the Rhetoric of Racism*, Jen McDaneld writes that Stanton implies black male violence is proof of her racism as it is correlated with a "misogynistic public discourse." Because Stanton made disparaging comments about black men, about their conduct and treatment of women, because of this she was deemed a racist by some. Stanton made the point that "if black men need the 15th amendment for protection, why don't black women need it as well."

Maybe the greater point McDaneld dismisses is that black women also could not own property, have custody of their children or have the right to marry. Rather than highlight these concerns, she includes statements like this, Stanton and those who did not support the 15th amendment, as the Revolution "stepped up its anti-black rhetoric, making references to the 'barbarism,' brute force,' and tyranny of black men." Ultimately, there was a split between those who supported the 15th amendment and, like Stanton and Anthony those who did not. Stanton said, "Our demand has long been suffrage for all, white and black, male and female, of legal age and sound mind."

There is no question Stanton and Anthony's paper, "The Revolution," which was the official publication of the National Woman Suffrage Association, which they formed, contained their frustration with the 15th amendment. Their intent was to secure all women's rights, black and white, through a federal constitutional amendment. In contrast, at the time Godey's Lady's Book had 150 thousand subscribers and was in business for 48 years, while The *Revolution* established by Anthony and Stanton, was active for four years from 1868 to 1872.

In 1850 Louis A. Godey wanted to improve his magazine with the hire of Sarah Josepha Hale as its literary editor, whose previous experience included 13 years as publisher of Boston's *The American Ladies' Magazine*. Mr. Godey was a conservative with strict policies against political intrigue in his magazine. He said, "I allow no man's religion to be attacked or sneered at, or the subject of politics to be mentioned in my magazine."

It's an interesting juxtaposition on politics in today's women's magazines from 2024, back to over a 170 years ago. In a ground breaking moment in 2015, *Glamour Magazine* announced they would publish a political section for 15 months called "The 51," a reference to the 51 million women under the age of 45 who will be eligible to vote in 2016." Vogue and Teen Vogue got political in 2016. For the first time in their history Vogue endorsed a Presidential candidate, Hillary Clinton. Vogue was founded in 1892, as a weekly high society journal. Teen Vogue was founded in 2003 as a sister magazine.

Aside from the antebellum woman's rights papers the *Lily*, the *Pittsburgh Saturday Visiter*, the *Genius of Liberty*, the *Una*, and the *Woman's Advocate* that Elizabeth Cady Stanton and Susan B. Anthony began and the *Revolution* in New York City in 1868, Lucy Stone a suffragist and activist began a rival paper in Boston in 1870, the *Woman's Journal. Sherilyn Cox Bennion* (Ph.D., Syracuse University) who was a professor of journalism at Humboldt State University, born 1935, published several articles about early women editors of the West. She provided in-depth portraits of nineteenth-century women editors of the

West and their diverse publications, and she identified at least twelve suffrage papers published in the West from 1869 to 1914.

Elizabeth Smith Miller was an advocate and financial supporter of the women's rights movement and a Suffragist. She introduced Amelia Bloomer and Elizabeth Cady Stanton to the short dress and Turkish trousers that would change the way women had dressed for centuries, which initially became the attire of women seeking reform. Referred to as the "Freedom Suit," to address feminism and dress reform in the U.S. in 1848-1875 and eventually the new style was referred to as the "Bloomer" and later it became known as the "freedom dress." For upper-and middle-class women especially, covered up for centuries in layer upon layer of fabric, dragging skirts in the dirt and rain, corsets that left one breathless, all for appearances sake, not for freedom of movement. Freedom suits go back to the 18th century in America and continued as slaves fought for their freedoms.

When Amelia Bloomer, a suffragist, began to promote dress reform in her magazine, *The Lily*, it reached its maximum circulation of four thousand, and its editors became synonymous with the reform costume. Ellet defended Bloomer's attire when a male friend accused Bloomer of dressing like a man. In contrast to *The Lily*, Godey's appealed to a broad audience of women and men that included supporters and opponents of Feminism. The circulation and popularity of Godey's Lady's book in comparison to the Lily demonstrates the opposition to women's rights in the 19th Century: *Lily* endured for seven years, Godey's Lady's Books for 68 years, from 1830 to 1898.

The *Una* founded by Paulina W. Davis, an American feminist reformer and a suffragist, who in 1853 owned one of the first *feminist* periodicals, written and edited entirely by women. In Caroline Dall's critique of Sarah J. Hale's first issue of the Una review of her *Woman's Record*, she voiced criticisms of Hale as a historian. *Caroline* Wells *Dall* (1822, 1912) was an American feminist writer, transcendentalist, and reformer. Dall quotes a portion of Hale's text in which she states that "she has no sympathy with those who are struggling on behalf of what are simply called woman's rights." Dall objected to Hale's depiction of the movement as beneficial for women only. Both editors Davis and Dall established the rhetoric of the movement by defining woman's rights as an issue of "human rights" that affects both women, and men in their society. Davis was President of the National Woman's Rights Central Committee from 1850 to 1858. In 1853, she began editing the women's newspaper *The Una*, handing over the responsibility to Caroline Healey Dall in 1855.

Chapter 15

On the Wings of Controversy Ellet Writes Women into History

Ellet's transformation, from house wife, at home writer, publishing posthumously at first, belonging to the "cult of Domesticity" to a professional writer commenced with some plucky moves for a 19th century female. Ellet immediately let people know she was in New York, locating herself amongst the New York Literati and associating with the literary nationalists, the "Young Americans," among them, Griswold, Simms and Duyckinck. During the time Poe's popularity ascended, she asked for an introduction, even sending him flirty notes to get his approval like most female writers. She went to various salons and wanted to "invite all the literati and famous artists," to her own soirees.

In this new literary world Ellet was now emersed in, it was a time when women were still seen as dependent and inferior to men. Griswold believed that intellectual women were not affectionate, and it was absurd to ignore the differences. Griswold and other male writers categorized female writers as "Veryblues" whose writings "inflicted, cruel and unusual punishment on American readers." Femininity was traduced as a quality which made women incapable of good writing, conversely women perceived men as incapable of writing for all audiences.

In Pursuit of Possibility, Elizabeth Ellet and The Women of the American Revolution, Gretchen Ferris Schoel's dissertation got this right when she included context, that Ellet wrote many "flirtatious poetic effusions" to Poe intended to win his "approval, not his romantic consent." One of Ellet's poems that she wrote to Poe called "The Coquette's Song" was published in the Broadway Journal in December 1845 when Poe was the publisher. The first stanza read:

> Ah yes, gentle sir, I will own I ne-er saw a perfection till now;
> That I never - no neve r- have known A smile such as your - I'll allow.
> And your eyes Oh, they speak to the soul
> With their glances as bright as the day?
> But I mean to keep my heart whole-
> So away with your love -vows-away.
> Away-Away- Away with your love vows- away?

From the EFE Jared Sparks folder at Houghton Library, Harvard University, "the more well-known Ellet had become, the more slander she experienced. Ellet did not feel compelled to defend herself against the slander and abuse of her peers." As of late 1886, an acquaintance warned that "[Ellet] would resent anything that looked like a personal attack on her. This behavior, however, was quite common among the New York elite." Two divergent views, one in opposition to the Poe's accounts and another by Jared Sparks and others. Ellet sought out Sparks when writing.

The Women of the American Revolution. Sparks was an American historian who published the George Washington's writings in twelve volumes, *The Writings of George Washington,* using primary sources from Washington's home in Mount Vernon, Virginia, as well as private and public archives.

Ellet became embroiled in a public battle with Rufus W. Griswold, whose dual marriages were the cause of Ellet and Ann S. Stephens testifying against Griswold in court in defense of his second wife, as did members of Griswold's deceased first wife's family.

The "scandalous" Ellet, as the Poe behemoth refers to her still, over 150 years later experienced some release after all the unfounded accusations, which allowed her to spread her literary wings and make new associations that propelled her interest in women's accomplishments with new publishing opportunities to new audiences.

It was another courageous career move for a female writer accused of gossip and slander against Poe, which did not impact her friendships with the women she had met at the Literati gatherings nor women fighting for equal rights, but it did change her career trajectory.

Ellet went on to publish about women in all types of roles and circumstances that necessitated change such as "Pioneer Women of the West," women adapting to a life that required them to do more than housework, and childcare, including some of the same jobs as men. In "Women Artists in All Ages and Countries," Ellet was introducing female artists as independent creators, yet she didn't challenge the concept of true womanhood, the roles of wives, mothers, or homemakers in more traditional sense. The focus was to provide a user-friendly text for women who likely never read the scholarly articles men wrote. In her book, *The Women of the American Revolution*, in three volumes, women's domestic chores became secondary to the role of becoming spies, messengers and female revolutionaries fighting alongside men in unheralded roles men never wrote about.

Few women wrote about history in the 19th century; history was only written by men. And we know that Griswold and Simms believed history was the domain of men. How remarkable when you consider women were writing history and politically involved in America in the 1700s. But what makes Ellet's history of the Revolution, entirely different, only women were the participants, even Washington, Paul Revere, Thomas Paine, and Thomas Jefferson, individuals most notably represented in America's early history, are not mentioned. Ellet is recognized today for accomplishments that in her day likely went unappreciated. Ellet's book, *The Queens of American Society* was "selected by scholars as being culturally important and is part of the knowledge base of civilization as we know it," according to Good Reads.

When Ellet wrote about women artists, and history writing, it was the territory of men and not a genre that women were known for. Ellet was compensating for omissions in women's creative endeavors and presenting it to a general audience, breaking through centuries of male only renditions of every facet of society, both current and historical. From poet to story, nature and history writer, Ellet had also become a populist writer focused on women in books like *The New Cyclopaedia of Domestic Economy and Practical Housekeeper, Family Pictures From The Bible* and *Queens of American Society.* Ellet also wrote *Watching Spirts,* at a time when spiritualism had become popular. Ellet corresponded with Margaret Fox Kane, one of three sisters in New York, who elicited a new found interest in spiritualism.

In a re-review by Sandra L. Langer of Ellet's book *Women Artists in all Ages and Countries,* which reflected on the history of woman's art and studies at a particular time in women's history, Langer concluded that Ellet could be considered a feminist and that her writing could be reviewed with that frame of perspective. Ellet's adherence to the expected, submissive roles of 19th Century women was part of her upbringing, but she changed as her passion for writing and acknowledgment of her work blossomed.

Ellet wrote and published *The Domestic History of the American Revolution, Pioneer Women of the West* and *Summer Rambles in the West*. Minnesota was a territory in 1849, opening up when railroads and canals, which brought a land boom in the 1850s. Ellet arrived in St Paul on the Ben Campbell steamboat in early 1850s. *Summer Rambles in the West*, is a travelogue, memoir of her own journey to parts of the country where European Americans were buying up land to farm and become their own bosses.

Chapter 16

Ellet Pioneering Women's History,
Feminist Scholarship

Ellet

Though it hasn't been a topic of discussion or research, Ellet's literary pursuits and her charitable assistance to women in desperate situations were supported by her husband, William Henry Ellet, a highly educated man who left a career as a professor and agreed to move back to New York to support Ellet's wishes. Not at all the norm for men of that era. Clearly, she loved him, as his death immobilized her.

Elizabeth Ellet came forward with this feminist revelation in the fall of 1847, "that the influence of women in the achievement of our national freedom has not been sufficiently shown. Our country really owes a debt of gratitude to the ladies who did so much to inspire the [Revolutionary] army and officers that had always been presented from a masculine perspective."

Ellet created a series of vignettes on *Heroic Women of the Revolution* for Godey's in 1847-48, and then went on to produce her three-volume series, *The Women of the American Revolution.* The first volume was published in 1848 or 1849. A critic noted, "Mrs. Ellet created an onstage female role in a historical pageant that had always been presented from a masculine perspective.

Elizabeth Fries Ellet in adulthood

Godey's Lady's Book publisher Sarah Josepha Hale combined the domestic and the heroic in Godey's engravings. Ellet described the difficulty of the Godey's project she did by saying, "The actions of men stand out in prominent relief and are safe in forming a judgment of them; a woman's sphere, on the other has been secluded, and in very few instances does her personal history, though she may fill a conspicuous position, afford sufficient incidence to throw a strong light upon her character."

Carol Mattingly's "Elizabeth Fries Lummis Ellet (1818-1877)," appeared in Legacy: A Journal of American Women Writers 18:1, 2001, which includes Ellet's task of recapturing women as active participants in the Revolutionary War, also revealing that her sources came from private letters and diaries, and from memories of those still living. Ellet quoted their own words and by referring to officer's letters, Ellet learned that officers complied with the direction of their wives, or their judgement.

In an excerpt from *The Woman of the American Revolution*, American Revolutionary women, Elizabeth, Grace and Rachel Martin, after being informed that a critical dispatch had to be delivered, two of the younger sisters put their husband's clothes on, and were given arms, to proceed to a station, where the road with a courier they would pass, but was guarded by two British officers. The bravery and resolve of American women living then went unnoticed by male historians.

In Pursuit of Possibility, Elizabeth Ellet and the Women of the American Revolution, by Gretchen Ferris Schoel, the most salient point made is that in a time of separate spheres, Ellet captured the historical truth, that women could do what men could do, that "women could claim public space and autonomous lives," that the "fluidity of social roles that existed in Revolutionary America could, indeed, characterize contemporary America."

In Ellet's *Women of the American Revolution*, North American Review, 1849, they write that "Mrs. Ellet has performed this not easy task with a care and patience which deserve to be called pious." Through my own wanderings into Ellet's history, even after creating an Interpretive Trail in her name, facilitated by internet communication, I am overwhelmed by her travels to museums and libraries, likely on a horse or carriages. Her contacts, which included the names of famous authors and historians, well known experts, including Jared Sparks, James Fenimore Cooper, and William Gilmore Simms.

Ellet's exploration of the American Revolution took her to historical societies of the North-east and the South, to scholars and descendants and experts also including Lydia Sigourney, the first women to make writing history into a business with her pen. Ellet also sought out Griswold on sources he had access to.

In 1849 the American Review wrote of Ellet's *The Women of the American Revolution* that this was a "simple record" of "the helpmeet of man," and in 1850 Graham's Magazine wrote it "brought directly home to the hearts... of readers."

Gretchen Ferris Schoel wrote as part of her MA thesis on Ellet that, "The possibility that Ellet pursued was that of a world in which she would be valued as an individual first and as a woman second. She ultimately found this world through her unique analysis of the American Revolution."

After reviews in Godey's, Graham's and Peterson's magazines and many other reviews, met with public approval, Ellet's task was considered one emblematic of "high moral duty," of someone with a "truly patriotic mind," and sentiments that were repeated like "Mrs. Ellet deserved to be called pious," in Godey's Lady's Book.

Ultimately, attacks came from Griswold and Simms that Ellet didn't give them enough recognition in her book following the book's publication. In the *Simms Review*, South Carolina, University, in speaking of Poe in reference to the Poe Ellet feud, he wrote that "any inklings of interference in his personal life by outsiders, who were not his personal friends, were not appreciated by Poe." Simms knew Ellet from South Carolina and helped her with her depictions of Southern women participants in the Revolutionary War. Simms's complaints that Ellet failed to give him credit for the idea of writing a book about women involved in the war of Independence, is so atypical of men in his era.

It is also true of Griswold, who granted Ellet access to the New York Historical Society, but he bemoaned that it was his idea to escort her there and became angry they she didn't give him more credit. Considering that he posited that women have never written a history book, based only on women's participation nor were they considered worthy of such an endeavor, nor were women allowed to write books at all, is why women's books were published posthumously under pseudonyms or anonymously. Ellet too published some of her early works anonymously. I would argue that male spheres, exclusion of female participation, entered into all aspects of life and the arts until the 20th Century.

After these male inspired incriminations and gossip circulated that Ellet was plagiarizing other's work. As the attacks progressed, Ellet wrote W.R. Lawrence, n.d., Hoadley Collection, Connecticut Historical Society. In this letter, Ellet is mentioning that she has been "booked" for a general reading but hopes that no one in New York will find out. *The Woman of the American Revolution* was published in 1848. W.R. Lawrence was a collector of autograph letters of famous people, which are now at the Armstrong Browning Library, and Museum. This identifies the antipathy toward Ellet circulating in New York resulting from the Poe, Osgood, Ellet drama.

Ellet wrote in the preface to her *Domestic History of the American Revolution*, "I cannot help believing too that a really better idea of the Revolution may be obtained from anecdotes in THE NEW ENGLAND QUARTERLY that exhibit the spirit which was abroad among all classes and which prompted to action than from the most accurate transcript of the maneuvers by which different battles were lost and won and the most precise statement of the number engaged or of killed and wounded on either side."

Ellet wrote about the contributions of women, and their husbands, like Mrs. Knox's husband, who was a Major General in the Continental Army and a close friend and advisor to George Washington. Henry is said to have counted on Lucy's opinions in matters concerning the conflict. Lucy's father was a loyalist to the Crown and Henry and Lucy Knox were patriots, so they left Boston together on Henry's horse.

Chapter 17

Ellet Writing in All Genres and Publications

In Early American Nature Writers, including Emerson, Thoreau, Audubon and Louis Hennepin, Kandi Tayebi writes about Ellet's life-long love of nature, beginning in Sodus Bay and how that love translated to her books, *Rambles About the Country* and *Summer Rambles in the West*. Ellet created pictures with words for every topographic change, people, customs and everyday experiences, all revealing themselves to people who had never traveled around the nation like Ellet. Here too in these discoveries was a different kind of encroachment, new settlers homesteading on the land Native Americans had lived for centuries. Tayebi wrote that it's true that students and those interested the 19th can find "information from her work never chronicled in such an effective way."

Ellet had a lifelong relationship with nature, which is reflected in her early poems and resurfaced in her book *Summer Rambles in the West*, a travelogue, memoir, one of the first by an American woman. Ellet brings the reader along on her journey with vivid descriptions, not just flora and fauna, but places and people she met on the way.

Ellet was also one the first women to write so extensively in three volumes, about women, when women's rights were still secondary to men's in The *Women of the American Revolution* in three volumes, published by Baker & Scribner, New York, first publication 1848. Throughout her book *Summer Rambles in the West*, she expressed disfavor for how men treated women. In one such occurrence in Minnesota when men set out to fish and hunt, they regarded a female going with them as an impossibility. Ellet's response was to question "why a woman couldn't keep her seat in a wagon as well as a man." Ellet considered it "masculine selfishness," in their refusal to allow women to share in the experience of this new place.

In her journey west to Minnesota, Ellet hiked the hills, boarded a flatboat or a carriage not in the fashions of the day, hoop skirts and breast-flattening corsets nor in Jenny Lind lace or crochet collars and full bishop sleeves, which were also popular then, along with print and checked fabrics, tiered cape-like jackets, and the fullest of skirts made of readily available cotton and linen. Ellet most likely did not wear hoops skirts and corsets on long excursions over muddy trails and camping out. Unlike most of the women, dressed in what Ellet described as "ball-room" attire of laces, short sleeves, delicate fabrics, and low necklines, and who were often confined to their cabins, Ellet wore "weather-defying ginghams," "delaines," and worsted wool, and took every advantage for herself and others to see and explore the natural environs through which she journeyed, as mentioned in my first book about Ellet, *Ramblings From The Trail, Wet Feet Soiled Dress and Defining Historical Truth*.

Anne Stephens was an American novelist and magazine editor. She is credited as the originator of the Dime Novel's genre. Ellet and Anne would have become acquainted at Botta's literary soirees. Both were frequently published in Dime Novels. The interest in Dime Novels came from the lucrative financial draw that even lured Alcott, Longfellow, Stevenson, and Tennyson. Filled with romantic and adventurous stories, Dime Novels were a precursor to modern paper back and comic books in the late 19th-century and early 20th-century providing fiction issued in series of inexpensive paperbound editions.

Ellet was a prolific writer and is known primarily for her books on women including:

Women Of the American Revolution 1, 11, 111
Pioneer Women of the West
Domestic History of the American Revolution
Women Artists in All Ages and Countries
The Eminent and Heroic Women of America
The Queens of American Society
Rambles About the Country
Summer Rambles in the West
The New Cyclopaedia of Domestic Economy and Practical
    Housekeeper
Family Pictures from The Bible
Watching Spirts
The Court Circles of the Republic

In "Early American Nature Writers," Kandi Tayebi wrote that despite Ellet's focus on women, "her historical work has not been recognized by feminist critics." Women living in the 19th Century and even beyond were not aware of Ellet's associations with women's rights and abolitionist leaders, but via letters and close acquaintances resulting in Ellet taking part in sheltering abused women, locating women lost and desperate and aggressively coming to the aide of women in difficult situations, none of which were widely publicized, so as to protect those women. All that and efforts by the Poe conglomerate have perpetuated an atypical attack on a female, who Poe had derided while living. Nevertheless, Ellet's contributions are revealed in this book, likely for the first time en masse, with the help of many historical dissertations and sources.

Chapter 18

*Ellet, A Career Path of Popularity and
Notoriety*

Recognized for the diversity and excellence of her writing by experts,
Ellet is acknowledged for poetry, nature writing, translations, women's
history, travelogue/memoir, books on domesticity, a children's book
and endless publications in dime novels, journals, magazines such as
Godey's Lady's Magazine, and her own publications, including her
600-page encyclopedia of American home economics, *The Practical
Housekeeper; The Domestic History of The American Revolution;
The Queens of American Society, Women of the American Revolution,
Pioneer Women of the West, Women Artists in all Ages and Countries,*
which are still studied today.

Ellet's poetry translations, her fluidity in different languages have
escaped the affirmative recognition she received for most of her contributions to history, with its clear-cut feminine interest.

Poe included Maroncelli, an Italian musician and poet among
his Literati. Maroncelli's poems, written in Italian, necessitating
translations. Either Poe was not aware of or ignored Ellet's poetry
translations of Maroncelli. Catharine Sedgwick aided Maroncelli,
who was a political exile and introduced him to New York circles,
including Ellet and Fitz-Greene Halleck, an American poet, essay-
ist, Byron scholar and member of the Knickerbocker group, who

both helped translate Maroncelli's "Addizioni" in Silvo Pellico's Le Mie Prigioni (Lograsso 785, 787n.29)

In Poe's Piero Maroncelli, he neglected to recognize that Maroncelli's poetry had appeared in the American Monthly Magazine and that another poem, "Hymn of the Night," which was also translated by Mrs. Ellet in the New York Mirror, and in a collection of Mrs. Ellet's poems.

Ellet was a superior linguist; and as her numerous and excellent translations attest to her proficiency in French, Italian, German and Spanish. Poe was also schooled in French, Spanish, Italian and German. A competitive air existed between them when it came to whose translation was correct, who was critiquing who, which was usually Poe and his supporters, making the topic of poetry translation by a women contentious, unacceptable, as was the case with Poe's perception of all of Ellet's writing.

Burton R. Pollin, CUNY Emeritus of English and honorary member of the Poe Studies Association, confers on his audience an assessment of Poe's "personal reasons" for avenging himself on Mrs. Ellet," who Beranger refers to as "one of the leading gossips of the New York literati." Evidently Poe and Ellet may have "crossed swords" over more than Poe's philandering and what Pollin referred to as the "swarming sisterhood of poetesses in the Lynch coterie who would applaud French Romanticism, as Ellet would not, which would have angered Poe.

Ellet's first book, *Poems*, Translated and Original, published in (1835), contained a collection of poems, many previously published, with translations from French, Italian, German, and Spanish. Ellet translated and published Silvio Pellico's Euphemio of Messina. And her tragic play, "Teresa Contarini," an original based on Venetian history, was performed in the spring of 1835 at the Park Theatre in New York City and smaller cities. Poe referred to this play as written in the "rifacimento" way, recasting, adapting and in a brief note he "charged her with wholesale plagiarism," yet admitted he felt no sufficient interest in her works, to investigate." Poe then described her as "short and much included to embonpoint." (plump, fleshy in the bosom). This came from a short note following another entry, which resided in the Berg Collection of the New York Public Library, as it was written, (May 25, 2019.)

In an undated July letter written to a Mrs. Field and Mrs. Osgood, Ellet asked if they were interested in publishing material, that she included in the second page of her letter. The return address went to Alexander Randall, in Elmira, New York. Randall was Governor of Wisconsin during the Civil War, who played a part in raising and organizing troops and was postmaster in Waukesha Wisconsin in 1845.

The offer to Osgood and Mrs. Field came from "The Original *Paradise Lost*, including *Adam and the Original Sin,* and a sacred drama from Andreini, Giovanni Battista, 1578: The complete poetical works of William Cowper...Milton, etc., and Adam, from the Italian. Ellet wrote that the work had never been translated into English, proposing to translate parallel passages from Milton to show how much he had borrowed and that no passages had ever reached this country. She wrote to Mrs. Field and Osgood, "We will make a volume of up to 150 to 400 pages. Illustrations would be furnished from original illustrations." This was not the act of a woman jealous of Osgood.

In two open letters from Thomas Dunn English to Mr. Ingram, Mr. Enlgish wrote:

"Looking back through a long life, of the many acquaintances who have passed away I remember few more worthy of respect [column 2:] and admiration than Elizabeth F. Ellet. She deservedly bore the reputation of a pure and estimable gentlewoman, while her ability as an author was more than respectable. Her *The Women of the American Revolution*, I, II, III and other works, were notable contributions to American literature at the time, and still have value. Poe's attempt to besmirch her spotless character, induced possibly by momentary vexation, was wickedly untrue; and you deserve, for reproducing it, the censure of all lovers of truth and honor."

The Women of the American Revolution Volumes I, II, III

Pioneer Women of the West

Domestic History of the American Revolution

Family Pictures from the Bible

Summer Rambles in the West

Queens of American Society

Rambles About the Country

The Eminent and Heroic Women of the Country

The Court Circles of the Republic

The Characters of Schiller

Love in a Maze, or the Debutante's Disenchantment

Poems Translated and Original

Scenes in the Life of Joanna of Sicily

Watching Spirits

My insight into Ellet's motivations and concerns go beyond what she wrote, and are best portrayed by what she didn't write, those ongoing private alliances and communications with women's rights leaders of the era to carry on her less public awareness of separate spheres and its impact on women's lives, and likely to remain a woman who could still make a living. This is evidenced in previous chapters. Context that's important and obvious is that Ellet's defenders, alive at the time, don't have a 24/7 loudspeaker, an online format used to defame Poe's critiques. If you want to know what derogatory comments, so-and-so said about Poe, you'll find it online at the Poe conglomerate's many portals of defamation.

As to Poe's mental health, and his accusations Ellet drove him insane, it's so much overkill, atypical of Poe. "In Reexamination of a Poe Date," Charles F. Briggs, original editor of the Broadway Journal, inserts Poe's response, "It is no wonder that I was driven mad by the intolerable sense of wrong?" It could be said, in consideration of Poe's penchant to blame others, that he was a great manipulator, blame shifting par excellence, even in his stories. Similar protestations are expressed by Rufus Griswold in his Statement of the Relations of Rufus Griswold, republished by Legare Street Press and now in the Public Domain.

Chapter 19

Poe's Epitaph

In the Poe, Griswold Controversy, by Killis Campbell, 1884, it becomes clear that Poe and Griswold's relationship revolved quickly into a competition. Once Poe vacated his position as editor of Grahams Magazine, Griswold became editor in his place. Poe's response was to retaliate by denigrating Griswold. On July 6, 1842 Poe wrote a correspondent at the South (Southern Literary Journal) that he intended, in a magazine that he was projecting, to "make war to the knife against the New England assumption of 'All the decency and all the talent' which has been so disgustingly manifested in the Rev. Rufus W. Griswold's *Poets and Poetry of America*. And it didn't end there, with "two anonymously written articles, both of which have been attributed to Poe, in which Griswold was held up to ridicule."

Two years passed before they spoke again, resulting in Poe "publishing praiseworthy notices in the Broadway Journal noting Griswold's editorial accomplishments." But their relationship continued to be off and on again. When Poe needed Griswold, often someone who Poe could depend on, for instance when he needed a loan of fifty dollars to keep the Broadway Journal afloat. But their relationship lapsed again according to Maria Clemm between 1846 and 1848. In 1848, Griswold published a critique of *The Raven* in *The New England Weekly Gazette*. In 1849 their relationship resumed with favorable notices they each wrote, Poe wrote a favorable notice of Griswold's *Female Poets of America,* and Griswold increased the number of Poe's poems in *Poets and Poetry of America.* After Poe's death, it came out that he had asked Griswold to be his literary executor.

Poe's early death at forty years old, October 7, 1849, in Baltimore, was recorded as "acute congestion of the brain," in simple terms, brain trauma. His demise has also been attributed to alcohol poisoning and other conditions and diseases, and some conjure he died of "cooping." He was found on a street in front of a bar, used as a polling place, on election day in Baltimore in clothes that were not his own, lending credence to the fact that he was used to vote multiple times, thus unknowingly committing voter fraud. He was dead four days later. A local paper wrote that he died of "congestion of the brain," which could describe being bludgeoned to death. More recently it's believed the real cause was encephalitic rabies.

There seems to have been no love lost between Poe and Griswold. In Poe's obituary, Griswold described Poe as a scoundrel and a madman, which was not out of line with Poe's already scandalous reputation. It would seem their tempestuous relationship, left scars of competitive aggression that never healed.

What's intriguing is the eventual whitewashing of his death by Poe contributors. In July of 1849, Poe went to the Old Swan Tavern delirious, Dr. George W. Rawlings said that Poe had drawn a pistol and tried to shoot him. After recovering from this incident, Poe joined a temperance society. By October third of that year, Poe was found unconscious near Ryan's Fourth Ward Polls, a polling place inside a public house, which corroborates with what has also been said by the Poe Society. Poe was taken to Washington Hospital where he died.

There is no telling of Poe's life or death that the Poe Society doesn't fault as misinformation, this is true of his final demise. All theories and explanations were bludgeoned, like the explanation from the Baltimore Clipper that Poe died of "congestion of the brain." In a more current assessment from a Public Broadcasting article, Poe's attending physician, Dr. John. J. Moran, stated Poe's cause of death was "phrenitis," (today's terms would be cephalitis, encephalitis, a virus associated with herpes simplex which alcohol consumption exacerbates). Surely the Poe Society could have picked up on that, instead they obscured potential contributing causes, which was that Poe died of alcoholism, which causes swelling or congestion of the brain. As previously mentioned, it wasn't until recently that Poe's death was attributed to encephalitic rabies.

There were no medical records or death certificates in those days, but any physician is likely to tell you, out of all of the scenarios the Poe Society refers to, without stating clearly that Poe wasn't just an alcoholic, he used opium, common in that era, which demonstrates their talent for obfuscating hard facts, accruing any unseemly behavior as the gossip of his detractors. What we do know from Poe's writing is the relationship between sex, death and the "feminine monstrous," aren't at all how we'd metamorphosize that describer of love into a real-to-life romantic love.

Griswold's Memoir discussed in *The Poe-Griswold Controversy,* by Killis Campbell, 1919, included six allegations referencing Poe's behavior, first at the University of Virginia, Poe led a destructive lifestyle of excesses, second after leaving college and enlisting in the US army and deserting his position, third that Poe was guilty of a crime in his relations with his second stepmother Mrs. Allen, fourth that some of Poe's publications were plagiarized, fifth, that his statements and opinions were under the influence of friend and foe, sixth that his life and his writings lacked ethics and principles. But then, Griswold was a consummate liar and traduced Poe after his death, even delegitimized Osgood's affections for Poe.

What is true today, is that some information has been riddled and shared by the Poe Society since 1923, filtrating thru books, articles and online formats, rendering an image of Poe that's a flattering depiction of a literary figure whose successes are forthwith in the conglomerate's receipts.

Initially Griswold's opinions were not disapproved of by Poe's defenders. As to the veracity of Griswold's statements, John R. Thompson, editor of the Southern Literary Messenger, said it was in his judgement, "truthful." Lewis Gaylord Clark, editor of the Knickerbocker, also concurred to the veracity of Griswold's commentary on Poe's demeanor.

There were other more damaging assessments by editors and a British critique and clergyman, but few public ones. One anonymous public review in the Saturday Evening Post in 1850 wrote he had "no very exalted opinion of Mr. Poe's character," but was unable to find any excuse for Griswold's course; and he suggests that Griswold probably understood literary executor to mean "one how executes."

George R. Graham, proprietor of Grahams' Magazine, which both Poe and Griswold edited, reviled Griswold's commentary as "unfair and untrue," calling it a "fancy sketch of a perverted, jaundiced vision, and ill-judged and misplaced calumny upon [a] gifted genius."

Also, "Graham was said to have written Mrs. Clemm in the fall of 1850 that he and others would come to Poe's defense." Graham later withdrew, his reason "in view of the decision of several discreet friends of the lamented Poe, he was withdrawing some letters and articles." Graham added that "the wounds made by his criticisms are too fresh-the conflicting interests too many, to hope to do that justice which time and sober second thought of educated minds will accord to his memory."

In August of 1853, an anonymous contributor to the Waverly Magazine, wrote of Griswold's Memoir, stating that an "unbiased life and collection of Poe's works" should be published. "In 1854, Graham published his second article in defense of Poe."

By 1852 a crowd of Poe devotees, who disagreed with Osgood's assessments of Poe, wrote in the Waverly, National, Russel's the Knickerbocker Magazines, the Godey's Lady's Book. A book published in his defense by Mrs. Whitman, *Poe and His Critiques* is accessible only at the Poe Blog at eaopoe.org. Note that they deemed Whitman as unreliable when it came to genealogical information and that she was a spiritualist. Which begs the question, why isn't it available on other research sites? Would that be attributable to their bias? Mrs. Whitman was once engaged to Poe, before she broke if off, after learning he had not stopped drinking and also due to her mother's disapproval of Poe. Mrs. Osgood reflected her agreement with Griswold in Poe's general behavior, which is a contradiction to her once laudatory praise of him, although Griswold was not an unbiased arbiter, except when it came to Poe's "chivalrous conduct toward women," whom he liked. Was Osgood speaking of the Bluestocking Literati, which included Transcendentalists, feminists and women writers who Poe was not physically attracted to and or those he generally demeaned because he disagreed with or disliked them? Two of the most critical writings after Poe's death by Griswold were the "Ludwig Article," and Griswold's Memoir of Poe.

In the "Contemporary Opinion of Poe" by Killis Campbell, he wrote that three judgements of Poe define truisms that prevailed, at least in 1920:

1. *That as a poet, Poe was not held in very high esteem by his contemporaries, and that he was virtually ignored by them until after the publication of The Raven in 1845.*
1. *That as a writer of gruesome and fantastical tales he early achieved considerable local fame, and that before his death he had come to be generally recognized as one of the leading writers of short stories in America.*
2. *That as a critic that he was chiefly known in his day and time in America, as fearless and caustic and not always impartial critic rather than as a just and discriminating critic.*

In the years following Poe's death his poetry was deemed as "extreme artificiality," while "containing little genuine feeling, and "an absence of all impulse," according to Griswold. This is not at all that dissimilar to what has been said about his poems by Virgnia Woolf and Dylan Thomas.

Despite many laudatory judgements, Campbell wrote, "But no one can read contemporary judgements on Poe without being convinced that he had not, at the time of his death, established himself in the minds of his own countrymen as a poet of extraordinary worth. It's equally plain that he had not attained any considerable vogue in foreign lands."

Most readers and critiques of Poe in the 21st Century would concur that Poe's genius is in his short stories. Killis agrees, he wrote, "As a writer of tales Poe fared a good deal better with his contemporaries than he did as a poet." What's truly astounding is that the first "tales" he wrote, submitting five in a competition offered by the Philadelphia Saturday Courier in 1831, were published anonymously. By 1832 they had not attracted much notice, the prize being awarded to a woman, a transcendentalist, social reformer, philosopher and historian, still accredited today as an American writer of plays and stories. Her name was one, you may not even know, Delia Salter Bacon, a Shakespeare Scholar. Poe submitted tales to the Baltimore Saturday Visitor in 1833 and was more successful, winning a prize and receiving public approval of the judges.

In the notes (William Cullen Bryant) "Bryant, after Emerson, among all American poets appears to have the least admiration for Poe, being blinded, I suspect, by his belief Poe was a bad man." When asked to raise funds in Poe's memory, Bryant wrote, "My difficulty arises from the personal character of Edgar A. Poe, of which I have in my time heard too much to be able to join in paying especial honor to his memory…"

Publisher H. C. Carey (Carey & Lea) one of the most important publishers in America at the time, wrote a letter November 26, 1834, saying that the "demand for such little things was slight and the produce from them small." Likely unknown to many is that *The Fall of the House of Usher,* praised by Washington Irving, and *The Gold Bug* were published before *The Raven*, which overshadowed both. Poe wrote his friend F.W. Thomas in 1845 that the "bird beat the bug all hollow."

Poe has had great success with his tales through time, but he's still known for criticisms he waged in an era of what are now acceptable isms, feminism, spiritualism, transcendentalism, philosophical movements that brought us out of the separate spheres mind-set of men. Albeit, not entirely, as they still exist in the 21st century. Of all the issues, his affair of the letters remains a feature the Poe Society continues to use to resurrect aspects of his character that historically are anti-feminist, particularly considering the strong female voices that emerged in the 19th century like Elizabeth Cady Stanton, Lucretia Mott, Harriet Tubman, Harriet Beecher Stowe, Susan B. Anthony, Sojourner Truth and writers like Margaret Fuller, Louisa May Alcott, Elizabeth Fries Ellet, Catharine Sedgwick, Emily Dickinson, and Ann S. Stephens.

Killis Campbell's contemporary sense of Poe is that he was generally ignored by his contemporaries in his lifetime, eventually gaining approval for his tales, attaining recognition as he reached the age of thirty-five. Poe died at the age of 40. But he did not have a greater following in his life-time due to these factors: his personal conduct, his apparent alcoholism and criticisms, which Americans could not, did not ignore in assessing him, even when considering his accomplishments as a writer. Killis wrote this in 1921, for perspective, The Poe Society formed in 1923.

Campbell came to these conclusions, using contemporary judgments which provide context versus the Poe's Society's versions:

1. *"That as poet Poe was not held in very high esteem by his contemporaries, and that he was virtually ignored by them until after the publication of 'The Raven in 1845."*
3. *"That as a writer of gruesome and fantastical tales he early achieved considerable local fame, and that before his death he had come to be generally recognized as one of the leading writers of short stories in America."*

4. *"That it was as critic that he was chiefly known in his day and time in America, though as a fearless and caustic and not always impartial critic rather than as a just and discriminating critic."*

5. *As to opinions of his work after his death, Campbell wrote, "widely appraisal without whole hearted commendation."*

6. *"In the Holden's Review. 22 Briggs wrote "All his poetry was mere machine work," and "Ripley in the New York Tribune, 23, declared that the particular characteristic of his poems was an extreme artificiality."*

7. *"In a notice by Willis in the Home Journal (October 27, 1849), in which he declared that The Bells, together with The Raven, Ulalume, and The Haunted Palace, afforded " unquestionably titles to an enduring reputation."*

8. *Campbell wrote that "out of all the contemporary judgments on Poe, the belief was at the time of his death, he had not established himself in the minds of Americans, as a poet of extraordinary worth."*

9. *As a writer of tales Poe was more successful with his contemporaries than with his poems. There was praise and dispraise as well, which focused on "his extravagances, the excess of the unnatural and the horrible."*

Epilogue

Up against a literary behemoth founded in 1923, endeavoring to rectify Poe's personal reputation as well as his contributions to literature, the Poe conglomerate, in many instances has inextricably separated the real-to-life Poe from their apotheosized version of him, by consistently highlighting Poe's preferred nemesis, as Elizabeth Fries Ellet, a tell-tale sign that they, like Poe continue to lash out at Ellet in defense of his womanizing and erratic and undisciplined behavior over 150 years later.

In James H. Whitty's *Memoir, The Complete Poems of Edgar Allen Poe,* Whitty wrote that Poe met Osgood at Lynch's weekly receptions, and that Osgood claimed their correspondences were for good and at the behest of his wife. Contrary to what Whitty wrote, after Ellet visited Poe's wife and saw the letters, Mrs. Virginia Poe must have disagreed and appealed to Margaret Fuller and Anne Lynch Botta to retrieve them. Poe's response was that Ellet should look after her own letters; one assumes he meant incriminating romantic letters. But none have ever been found, but it's the reason why Kelly Keener, a Poe affiliate, purchased the Ellet Autograph Album for the Poe Society over 150 years after Poe's death to validate the lost letters that have the lasting potential to defame Ellet. But Kenneth Silverman, author and Pulitzer Prize recipient wrote in his book, *Edgar A. Poe, A Biography, Mournful and Never-Ending Remembrance,* there were no such letters.

To provide some context, Whitty wrote that Ellet, Lynch, Whitman, et al, sought him out for different reasons. Many of those letters "have been lost sight of," Whitty writes. What he fails to mention, Poe was the editor and sole owner of the Broadway Journal in 1845, it's likely hundreds of women sought his praise, meetings and publication of their work, many with a flirtatious air, not necessarily inferring a romantic interest, positive reviews and publication for a price, which has not been highlighted by the Poe Society.

Women writers who wanted to be published in the Broadway Journal, including laudatory critiques from Poe, was the bulk of his following. *In Women's Place in Poe Studies*, author Eliza Richards wrote that though Poe was an adept, astute critique, but when it came to women, his judgement was colored by physical attraction or by being paid to "puff them." It's clear Poe's relationships with female writers, who he defended, defended him in return, even after his death.

The newest reveal, that Ellet wrote Osgood in her apology for the gossip that ensued after the affair of the letters, is of the existence of a "fake letter." Through information gathering there are substantial implications of interference by Maria Clemm, Virginia Poe's mother, which has not been fully recognized by the Poe Society. The letter referring to a fake letter was written By Ellet to Osgood in her July (7) 8,1846 after Samuel Osgood threatened to sue Ellet.

Whether Ellet had romantic interests, envious motives or not, from all indications, particularly her own written words in her Ramblings Travelogue, Memoir, Ellet disdained male authoritative presumptions throughout her life, refusing to accept boundaries. Ellet defended and supported women, wrote about women and came to their aid in all manner of assistance. She was outspoken and independent, in fact Pulitzer Prize winning Author, Kenneth Silverman, in his book, *Edgar A. Poe, A Biography, Mournful and Never-Ending Remembrance,* referred to Ellet as "formidable and knowledgeable," just the type of female Poe and now the Poe conglomerate would have every reason to continuously kill off, reputationally and allegorically!

Author's Note

I moved to Eden Prairie twenty three years ago and like Ellet, who described in her 1852 travelogue as the garden spot of the territory, the version I saw 149 years later was replete with corn fields and a never-ending vision of nature in the wild.

Back then the talk in Eden Prairie usually included Elizabeth. I was fascinated as a newcomer and identified with her, because I too walked her walk in a place where nature is everywhere. In 2021, in an article in Eden Prairie News, I wrote this about Elizabeth: "She was very inquisitive and adventurous and insatiable…much different than women back then. They were all dressed up in pointed shoes. What was Ellet doing? She was out there camping. And sleeping in a tent and suffering through mosquitoes."

After obtaining the only version I could find of Summer Rambles in the West, a ringed binder republished by University of Minnesota containing Ellet's visit here and my first introduction to the real Ellet in her words, I contacted my Hamline friend and author Susan Thurston to be my editor.

Now, a second book on Ellet will be on the shelves soon. Susan and I have made this journey together and I doubt Susan can count all my phone calls and emails, me relaying my amazement in discovering who the real Ellet was, not the one her male detractors made her out to be.

How many times did Susan hear me say, "you're not going to believe this..." and it continued like that, discovery after discovery. It was the experience of a lifetime and I will never forget what I regard as the most telling, accurate reveal of who Elizabeth Fries Ellet was.

Vicki Pellar Price

About the Author

Vicki Pellar Price is the director of Writers Rising Up to Defend Place, Natural Habitat, Wetlands (since 2001). The 501 (c) (3) literary nonprofit is based in Eden Prairie. The Elizabeth Fries Ellet Interpretive Trail was a four-year project the non-profit undertook to create a permanent guide to Eden Prairie's history and natural biomes in a 125-acre stretch of untouched prairie, big woods, sedge meadow, oak savanna and bottomland forest. The non-profit has partnered with the Arboretum on writing workshops and readings related to place and natural habitat with Minnesota writers Carol Bly, Bill Holm, Paul Gruchow, Deborah Keenan, Joyce Sutphen and Michael Dennis Browne. Pellar Price has a BFA from California Institute of the Arts (Chouinard Art Institute), and MLA & MFA from Hamline. Pellar Price is the author of *Ramblings from the Trail*, *Wet Feet*, *Soiled Dress*, *Defining Historical Truth* and her new book, *The Indomitable Elizabeth Fries Ellet- Feminist: Defining Historical Truth of the Nineteenth Century*.

www.ingramcontent.com/pod-product-compliance
Lightning Source LLC
Chambersburg PA
CBHW030825090426
42737CB00009B/874